A MAGIC DWELLS

A Magic Dwells

A POETIC AND PSYCHOLOGICAL STUDY

OF

THE NAVAHO EMERGENCE MYTH

BY

SHEILA MOON, PH.D.

Wesleyan University Press

MIDDLETOWN, CONNECTICUT

ISBN: 0-8195-4018-8

Library of Congress Catalog Card Number: 72-105501

Manufactured in the United States of America

FIRST EDITION

Dedicated to
Linda Fierz-David
whose wisdom about
myths and mysteries
is woven into every
page of this book

As every blossom fades and all youth sinks
into old age, so every life's design,
each flower of wisdom, every good, attains
its prime and cannot last forever.
At each life's call the heart must be prepared
to take its leave and to commence afresh,
courageously and with no hint of grief
submit itself to other, newer ties.
A magic dwells in each beginning and
protecting us it tells us how to live.

—HERMANN HESSE
(from *Magister Ludi*, tr. M. Savill,
[London and New York, 1949] p. 396.)

Contents

Acknowledgments

I wish to acknowledge my gratitude and indebtedness to Dr. Paul Radin, Mrs. Linda Fierz-David, and Mrs. Emma Jung, all deceased, for their help and invaluable advice when I was working on this manuscript; to my friends Dr. Elizabeth B. Howes, Miss Florence Little, and Miss Luella Sibbald for support along the way; and to Miss Maud Oakes for the availability of some of her material. In Santa Fe, New Mexico, I was extended many courtesies and the full use of the library and archives of the Museum of Navaho Ceremonial Art. I also wish to thank the Bollingen Foundation for the grant which enabled me to undertake this work.

S. M.

A MAGIC DWELLS

Foreword

BECAUSE I believe in the efficacy of poetic and mythic statements to carry their burdens without much sounding of horns, I would have preferred this less poetic (and probably more pedantic) part of the book at the end. For those who find this sort of explanation dull, it need be no disturbance. They may step over it. For those who want such an introduction, here it is. (I confess I am one of those unpredictable readers who sometimes want explanations and sometimes don't.) I have tried to tell why I wrote this book, from what point of view I wrote it, and about the people to whom the myth and its magic originally belonged.

This is a book about a myth—the Navaho Indian creation myth—about meanings of myth, and about the relevance of myths and their meanings to the psychological-religious growth of the individual personality. We in America have a wealth of indigenous myths which have for centuries carried the meanings of man, but this richness we have largely ignored as we have ignored most values offered by the American Indian. My concern was to present part of a single body of material—the Emergence myth —of one Indian group: the Navaho of the southwest United States. My purpose, both as a writer and as a psychotherapist trained in the analytical psychology of C. G.

Jung (and believing his to be the fullest and richest psychological approach to such material), was to set forth a selected sample of the content and symbolism of a great religious tradition and to discuss and interpret it as a source of illumination for the darkness in the spirit of man.*

Cosmic myths such as the Navaho creation are, as Dr. Jung indicated, dreams of mankind. They contain symbols and symbolic situations relating to man's spiritual search for himself. In our time man is lonely and lost; his meanings are obscured, his myths sentimental and second-rate; and he needs the great dreams for his survival. While cultural evolution, as well as personal development chronologically viewed, is reflected in such cosmic myths, my conviction grows that the myths touch levels of meaning more basic than personal or cultural, that they speak to contemporary man as articulately as to his forebears of suprapersonal realities and of ultimate destinies. We can assume that man's needs for individual meaning and value are expressed in his myths as in his outer social strivings and, further, that myths can be psychologically "explained" as man's symbolization of processes which seek to re-establish harmonies both within himself and between himself and others.

We can put it another way. There are universally or almost universally experienced situations occurring in the life progression of everyone (such as birth, speech, death). To misunderstand or to understand them conditions most subsequent situations. Myths are tries for understanding; when really alive and functional they are more satisfactory tries than most intellectual systems. Even when a myth is wrenched from its original psychological earth and misused, as in the case of the Wotan myth in Nazi Germany,[1]

---

* This is not a general book about American Indians; nor is it a general treatment of the Navaho Indians, their chants, prayers, songs, sandpaintings, culture. Many such volumes are available, written by experts in archaeology, physical and cultural anthropology, sociology.

it has undeniably great power. And when a myth is seen in its rightful and natural setting and is related not to a prejudiced schema (as Hitler's), but to the psychology of personal development, its powers to stir the heart and clarify the mind are unbelievably strong.

As psychotherapist and psychologist, I know it is important for men and women to try to understand themselves. Dreams, fantasies, myths—all are valuable sources of insight. They personalize and personify aspects of the personality, thus making it more possible for the individual, if he wishes, to be objective about himself. I have seen this empirically tested, not only in my psychotherapeutic practice but also in the countless discussion groups I have led and college and university classes I have taught. For about twenty-five years now such groups have discussed the personal application of myths, and in the interpretations given, my debt to these discussion groups is no small one.

In this book I am talking of the human personality as I feel the myth is describing it. Whatever psychological and religious statements I make are based on my perceptions of the *as-if* situations in the myth checked against my empirical data. This way of approaching myth is not a spurious psychological activity of imposing meanings where none in fact exist. The authors of *The Navaho* write:

> Mythology is the response of man's imagination to the uncharted areas of human experience. . . . Folklore must be presumed to originate in the dreams and phantasies of individuals. But when the product of one person's imagination (as mingled with and modified by the phantasy of other persons over a long period) is taken over as a part of the mythology of the whole group, the themes may confidently be assumed to correspond to widely current psychological situations.[2]

These situations, I believe, are not so much outer as inner processes, related to what Jung has called *archetypes*, by which he means psychologically necessary and innately potential responses to a variety of life situations. Archetypal motifs and situations, the very core of great myths, are individually lived (although they may affect entire cultures). And despite what one usually believes about so-called "primitive" man and his immersion in his group, the Navaho is deeply concerned with individuals.

> The Navaho's interest is focussed upon restoring the harmony within an individual and between that individual and other persons or supernatural forces. The Navaho outlook is more personal. . . . The individual counts for a very great deal in the Navaho way of thinking.[3]

And who are these Navaho people? For over a thousand years they have lived in the southwestern United States, probably having migrated from the north and possibly, thousands of years earlier, from the Orient. During their prehistoric period they were doubtless enriched and vitalized by contact with other tribes, particularly Pueblo groups. They are today the largest American Indian group and are increasing despite most difficult economic and geographic conditions. (For detailed accounts of their history, see Kluckhohn and Leighton, and others.) Their mythology, art, religion, and psychology are inextricably entwined.

> The white world is now mainly a secular world. As clerics so often complain, white people "turn religion on and off." They may go to church on Sundays and a few other occasions. Births, marriages, and deaths are usually solemnized, but most whites do not feel that religion has anything to do with large sectors of life. With the Navaho it is quite different. Their world is still a whole.[4]

This wholeness of the Navaho universe is reflected in the fact that all their many myths and chants ultimately can be seen to be offshoots of their Emergence story, or origin myth. Wyman writes:

> Among the myths already published, the basic tale and closest analogue to the Judeo-Christian Bible is the Emer-

gence story. . . . The origin myths of most ceremonials stem from facets of this basic myth, each being elaborated as a more or less separate story.[5]

Reichard,[6] Kluckhohn,[7] and others have also pointed out this centrality and sacredness of the origin myth. The age of the origin myth cannot yet be known, nor can it be determined to what extent it was originally influenced by Pueblo Indian myths or, before that, by archaic Oriental sources in the remote past. Inasmuch as the Navaho language has not had a written form (except as devised by modern investigators), the many extant versions of the origin myth have come from verbal accounts given by older members of the tribe. Each informant has shaped his version in his own particularized fashion. Of the twenty or more recorded versions, most are brief, sketchy, or from rather questionable sources. A few, notably the Matthews, Wheelwright, and Haile versions, are full and comprehensive. The Haile version is the basis for this book, both because Father Berard Haile was a highly skilled linguist and thus produced trustworthy records and also because this version is particularly fascinating for its interplay of "light" and "dark" powers, inasmuch as it is the Emergence told from the "evilway" side.[8] (At the end of Chapter VII, there is a complete paraphrase of the Haile version of the Emergence myth. Also, each chapter of the book, and each subchapter, begins with a similar paraphrase of the relevant Haile material. All such synopses are in my own words. Occasional direct quotations from Haile are so marked.)

I have tried to set forth this myth and to put together the artist's perception and the psychologist's perception, whether in presenting and interpreting the Emergence story, in giving examples from my psychological practice, or in summarizing various comparative mythological sources. In psychotherapy, one's individual myth speaks thus, alternating between subjectivity and objectivity, between emotional responses to inner symbols and conscious understanding of them. The cosmic preforms, the eternal presences, the archetypes, move man, fill him with awe and wonder, make him "know" in a different fashion. This is the "heart-mind" language, some of which, I hope, is present in this book. Possibly some of the wonder and fear and loveliness which I knew in feeling my way into the myth may be communicated.

I

Prologue

In the beginning, in the small and the great darkness, life is not Something; it ardently Is. Beginnings are not precision. Beginnings are not confusion. They are darkness drawn to a minute point of nondarkness, and silence gathered into a small sound. What is gathered and drawn together, and who gathers and focuses, lies behind knowledge. Man can only know, as he peers into the mystery, that it is so. And in his own way he has tried since his earliest history to say that it is so.

Lying under the earth, the walls of Magdalenian caves carry the spontaneous expressions of beginnings. The ballets of animals moving in the darkness of the caves are meanings illuminating the silence. The cool and remote megaliths of Avebury and Stonehenge pull at the dawn with new fingers after thousands of years, and the darkness is lifted on another beginning. More explicitly and fully than these things, the cosmic creation myths of mankind sing the song of what is and can be. Their origins, as all origins, recede and are lost in the depth of time. But through the faithful wondering and work of generations, they have been shaped and structured and passed on to us, full to bursting with the voices of man's awareness of himself. They are in this sense man's own creation from his interior knowing, his important gift to his successors.

Who among us can say that the vision of beginning and becoming has left us when we let ourselves be gripped by the ebb and flow, the rise and fall, the absorbing contrapuntal music of these mythic tellings? We must listen— and the answer must wait on the hearing. For it is the sound of our own life moving in us, out of the small darkness of our own beginnings.

It must never be forgotten that man is far more than his consciousness. He is his darkness also. He is a being with a magnitude of unconscious dimensions and levels forever at work in him. Where he builds masks and walls to conceal himself from himself, just there is the pain of the pressures of unfulfillment. Where he tries bravely and poignantly to be what he is not, to disregard his deepest desires, just there is neurosis and emptiness. What man most needs is the unconscious "others" in himself. What he does is to dismiss them as nonsense, or at best to spend guilty moments with them—moments snatched from the much more important business of getting ahead.

Psychological or religious redemption is the act of recovering for oneself out of the small dark beginnings an essential value or values which one knows to be one's own and also recognizes as having been lost. A genuine longing for this lost treasure is in no sense "escapism," although the treasure is sought for in many psychologically unsound ways—philanthropy, asceticism, spiritualism, occultism— as ends in themselves. But time and again men have returned to the true search, and since the first "once upon a time" the great world myths and fairy tales have been concerned with it. The same search has been described by psychologists (by Jung in all his work), by philosophers, by theologians (see the writings of Paul Tillich), by artists (as in certain statements by Miró, Kazantzakis, Pasternak, and others). All these have been concerned with the great deep of the human soul and with the meaning of existence. So is the myth.

The way of redemption is basically a paradox, as are

many truths. The paradox of the search as it appears in this version of the Navaho myth, as well as in many other myths and in human experience, can be stated simply. Only through darkness, chaos, the unformed, the difficult, can light come into being. This is the vision of redemption. It is a vision with deep roots in the human psyche, a vision of true consciousness and wholeness, a vision of ultimate unity which contains within it the duality of existence.

Myth is one way through which we rootless moderns can re-evaluate ourselves and our relation to the universe. In myth, man has articulated his insights about his own meaning. The outlines of his destiny are drawn in his folklore, as it in turn has been shaped by the outreach of his creative mind and spirit. But to talk about myths and mythic symbols and their meanings, valuable though this is, is not enough if we are looking for a personal relationship to the myth. We need, in addition to knowledge about and empathy for these myths, some sense of why and how they relate to us in our specific time-space framework.

Some sort of world view is either explicit or implicit in all myths of creation. In a greatly oversimplified manner, let us say that there are two major types of world view, or two major ways of approach to the "meaning of life," which is after all the subject matter of cosmic myth. These may be variously labeled: Oriental and Occidental, aesthetic and theoretical,[1] or world and life negation and world and life affirmation.[2] The Oriental way values the immediately given experience, timelessness, the aesthetic component, the inner perfection of being. It tends to find the outer world more or less negative and meaningless. It is generally more "natural" and less ethical than is the Occidental way. The latter places far greater emphasis on the inferred, the theoretical adventure into the future. The world as such is more meaningful, time is more highly valued, as is outer change. The Oriental way concerns itself with eternity, the Occidental with time, although each is continually being confronted with its opposite. The marked dualistic

tendencies of the West are in part due to this preoccupa-
tion with time, as it seems easier to bring time into eternity
than to pull eternity into the time-bound world. Perhaps
modern man needs to find a new balance. Surely we of the
Occidental world are desperately limited in natural responses to the immediately given and in emphasis on the
inner perfection of being.

This Emergence story is an expression of both an
Oriental and an Occidental world view. It is primarily concerned with man's emergence from the world of darkness
into the state of being Man, that is, with the problem of
redemption. The slow, patient climb upward is in terms of
the immediately given and the natural. No real dualism is
anywhere evident; and in this the myth is surely Oriental.
But there are also present both a reaching into the future
and an element of striving for a better life for men, which
are more Occidental emphases. Being an American, with
roots down in my land, I must bring those myths arising
from the American continent. Strange though they seem at
first, however, their strangeness is only of a partial kind.
The same archaic wisdom moves in them as moves in other
better-known myths. The same need to understand stirs
them. The same tie to the spirit of man makes them valid.

How this Navaho myth has come to be such an impressive combination of psychological-religious elements is a
question which perhaps can never be fully answered.
Surely the North American country where the Navahos
have lived for the past centuries has contributed much to
the myth's richness. Its vast, beautiful, lonely spaces, the
sharp and impersonal mountains, the sky of unearthly blue,
all must have encouraged an intense inwardness. Yet also
this landscape has an expansiveness not often experienced;
not a warm expansiveness, but an almost cruel challenge
which pulls always toward the next mesa, the farther butte.
Moreover, it is a fairly well accepted theory that originally
these North American Indians came from Asiatic lands.
Perhaps some of the Oriental qualities of the myth derive

from this. In the final analysis, however, the uniqueness of the Emergence myth can be "explained" only after much more is known about the Navahos (and about the Zuñi and Hopi to whom their myth owes much), not only anthropologically but spiritually. Even then the essential mystery will probably remain, as it is the same mystery about the human spirit which eventually lies behind the ultimate questions.

As I have said, myths are interpreters of the depths of man, carriers of the life values, dynamic movements from timelessness and spacelessness into human time and space. And as with other creation myths, so it is with those of the American Indians: a mirror is held for the psyche of man to look into and to see how it is with him. For the image of man is far more than his surface. He is deep upon deep of richness and despair, of laughter and demons, of animals and angels. And he must know and relate to these depths if he is to fulfill his implicit divinity. To seal them over as a dry well is to assure his ultimate death.

Let us go, then, into the vastness of sky and earth which is Navaho Indian country—and into the great and the small darkness of the beginning of the Navaho Emergence myth.

II

Forms and Images

Summary
CREATORS AND CREATED

In the first dark underworld nine people lived: six kinds of ants, three kinds of beetles. At each of the four directions—north, south, east, west—was a round house like an anthill four stories high, with chiefs at each corner of the world. All the people spoke the same language. There were no stones nor any vegetation nor any light.

After a discussion among the chiefs, in the center the people built a house of four chambers, one above the other, and moved from the lowest room up to the next one.

HERE the work commences; the fascination of the making of a beginning, of the rise of consciousness, is at hand. All is darkness and timelessness. "There were no stones nor any vegetation nor any light." Only the soft clicking of beetles and the soundless motion of ants disturb the dark and the silence. The goal is dim and misty, for the start of creation here is only a movement and not at first a direction. This is one of the most primitive—in the sense of undifferentiated—of all tales of beginnings. Elemental and primal, it nonetheless has activity and a sense of energy having cohered about several definite nuclei: the insects. From these nuclei, development begins.

Testimony for the universality of an awareness of what beginnings are like is given in various ways, showing various facets, by other creation stories. For the Egyptians, life emerged from the formlessness and "inertness" of the abyss.[1] Babylonian myth tells of the time when there were no heavens, no earth, no gods—only the great waters mingling together in Chaos.[2] This same Chaos—which, according to Bayley,[3] was space rather than confusion and which existed previous to the creation of the universe—figures in many cosmogonies. Floating masses of vapor were the beginning of things, said the Burmese Kachins.[4] The Zuñi of North America pictured creation beginning out of fog "rising like steam." [5] Spence tells that the Peruvian concept was that "in the year and the day of the clouds, before ever were years or days, the world lay in darkness. All things were odorless, and a water covered the slime and ooze that the earth then was." [6]

Water is a primal substance, not only in these and in the Old Testament account but also in the beautiful description in the *Popol Vuh* of the Quiché Mayans.[7] This is the account of how all was in suspense, all calm, in silence; all motionless, still, and the expanse of the sky was empty.

> The surface of the earth had not appeared. There was only the calm sea and the great expanse of the sky. There was nothing brought together, nothing which could make a noise, nor anything which might move, or tremble, or could make noise in the sky. There was nothing standing; only the calm water, the placid sea, alone and tranquil. Nothing existed. There was only immobility and silence in the darkness, in the night.[8]

Norse myth has a lean but fine description of what lies at the origins of things.

> In ancient days
> existed nothing,
>   neither sand nor sea
>   nor swelling billows;
> there was no earth
> there was no heaven
>   not a blade of grass
>   but a Yawning Gulf.[9]

This sense of mingling waters, immobility, silence, darkness, the unfilled void, is well known to any woman who has conceived but has not yet felt the life within her move. It is known also to anyone who is waiting for change, in that motionless state before change begins. It is as if, although one knows better, nothing had "created" anything, but yet something is there—or could be there—below the sea, the silence, the stillness, and the shadows. Where is the creator? one cries soundlessly. Who fills this void? Who vitalizes this inert mass?

The Old Testament myth[10] has a creator-god who stands at the beginning and says, "Let there be light!" This marks one major difference between the Judeo-Christian and the Navaho orientation and surely emphasizes the higher consciousness of the Judaic myth, a difference of emphasis which will be seen more clearly later on. In Genesis, God begins to work very soon on nature as His material. Even so, according to the Old Testament myth, "the earth was a desolate waste, with darkness covering the abyss and a tempestuous wind raging over the surface of the waters."

Thus, when one stands in the "darkness, in the night," where is "nothing brought together," there is no creator-god, no one to call for light. At such times, in such myths as the Navaho Emergence, the first polarity is tale versus teller. The creator is the telling—as a man may whisper to himself in his aloneness, or may share with another his shadowed fears, and from the sharing, life is born. When, as in the present myth, nature and night, rather than a creator-god, come first, the potential achievement of the spirit is both a magnet which draws the substance into a pattern and also the material for patterning.

A vivid example of the polarity of potential is found in the Arizona Pima Indian myth.

In the beginning there was only darkness everywhere—darkness and water. And the darkness gathered thick in places, crowding together and then separating, crowding and separating until at last out of one of the places where the darkness had crowded there came forth a man. This man wandered through the darkness until he began to think; then he knew himself and that he was a man; he knew that he was there for some purpose. . . . Then he made for himself little ants.[11]

Let us return to the beginning of Navaho myth, to the ants and beetles. Here the uncreated ones are stirring about and sensing out the dimensions of their darkness. Here Mother-night-and-nature is the first bearer of the implied meanings, for contained in her are the insects, the primal, undifferentiated, restless, creative tensions. Curtin, in an early work on American Indians cosmogonies, referred to "self-existent personages or divinities" at the beginning. Such divinities, he wrote, "were everything at first; there was nothing except them, nothing aside from them, nothing beyond them." They existed, as he pointed out, in a "chaos of quiescent mind" which remarkably resembled, or was analogous to, the undifferentiated matter which, "according to the nebular hypothesis, filled all points of space in the physical universe before the first impulse of motion was given to it." [12] There is also a quite elaborate and abstract concept of the Dogon of Africa which further emphasizes how, from the undefined stirrings within the cosmic mother womb, life is beginning:

The original germ of life is symbolized by the smallest cultivated seed—*Digitaria exilis*—commonly known as fonio and also called by the Dogon *Kize uzi*, "the little thing." This seed, quickened by an internal vibration, bursts the enveloping sheath, and emerges to reach the uttermost confines of the universe. At the same time this unfolding matter moves along a path which forms a spiral or helix. . . . Two fundamental notions are thus expressed; on the one hand the perpetual helical movement signifies the conservation of matter; further, this movement . . . is held to represent the perpetual alternation of opposites—right and left, high and low, odd and even,

male and female—reflecting a principle of twinness, which
ideally should direct the proliferation of life. These pairs
of opposites support each other in an equilibrium which
the individual being conserves within itself. On the other
hand, the infinite extension of the universe is expressed by
the continual progression of matter along this spiral path.

These primordial movements are conceived in terms of
an ovoid form—"the egg of the world" (*aduno tal*) within
which lie, already differentiated, the germs of things.[13]

Is it not in some such way, too, with the start, for each
of us, of our self-awareness, whether in our body's infancy
or in the childhood of our personality? We know nothing;
we are nothing clearly defined; our goal is a question. Our
inner world is a vagueness of moving forms and figures,
with no present sense of having been created. The ger-
minal seed, the "little thing," the insect, is vibrating. We
sense, we desire something, and in this tormenting desire
are life and energy, the bursting of the sheath.

A first structuring is there in the Navaho myth in the
round four-storied houses at the four corners. In their
tetradic directionality lies the intimation of the spirit's
pull outward and upward, similar to the Dogon unfolding
spiral. Primitive man, in the naming or making of such a
four-sided figure or mandala, involves himself in that which
comprises the seeing of his own wholeness. The equal-armed
cross is a testament even in the cave dwellings of the dawn
men. How many crossroads, benign or malevolent, are
stumbled upon by the wanderers in fairy tales and myths,
to demand a focus of restless searching? The outer life
of the race has for untold ages been oriented about the
cycles of the seasons; the vastness of the earth, the sea,
the sky—charted about east, west, north, and south. Is
it so different with the inner life of the individual? Here
as well there surely are seasons of planting and seasons of
gathering in, seasons of quiet germination when the sap
runs slow, and seasons of prodigality. And there is the
rising of new meanings over and over as the sun rises in the

east, the always mysterious lure of unknown norths and the shattering of storms, the south of the warm fullness of existence, the goldenness of westerly respites.

What better way could the unconscious process in man choose to symbolize the wholeness of nature than in this quiet quiescent horizontal mandala of the four mounds at the four compass points. Yet something is lacking. Only the nervous excitement and restlessness of the ants and the beetles are there. (Insects are the first beings present in the Washington Matthews version of the Emergence also, where ants, dragonflies, beetles, and locusts lived in the first world surrounded by water.[14] And in Zuñi ritual, an "ant-entering place" and an "ant-place" are mentioned prior to the "Middle place" [15]). In the myth a center is missing; a focal point for the creation is not there. Yet a fundamental necessity, before we can be aware of ourselves and our meaning, is a center from which our ordeal of exploration can radiate.

Thus the urgent need is born for that which creates. Some myths express this only as a general motif of self-originating Beings who do the work of creation,[16] or as a mating of ocean with some spirit force,[17] or as a kind of divine emanation.[18] A more definite creator, deliberating and making, is described by other myths. An early form of this is found in certain Inca myths which, according to Spence,[19] told of a powerful spirit who made things be. In its first manifestation, however, this image was not that of a direct creator-ruler, but rather that of a pre-existing creative agency, *Conticsi-viracocha* (He who gives Origin, or Beginning). Many American Indian groups have similar fairly well defined creator-gods. The Wishosk[20] tell of Above-old-man who, out of the nothingness of earth, made man. "He merely thought and they existed." Earthmaker, in the great Winnebago myth,[21] first came to consciousness, made light, decided to create something good, finally "created a world on which to sit and exist." Kumush, Old Man of the Ancients, is the Modoc creator,[22] while

Cushing[23] describes the Ancient Father of the Sun of the Zuñi. All these creator-gods, despite differences in structure, in precision, in focusing power, are centers from which spiral movements begin.

To know ourselves is a simple and terrible thing, needing above all a secure place on which our feet can be planted. Yet perhaps it is first the sense of points in the vagueness, and the urgent and irritable motion this sense arouses, that sharpens the drive toward centering and framing the experience. We are stirred up, we say. We feel at sixes and sevens, or at odds with our life, we say. In short, we know something of these dark and unfocused beginnings if we but listen. One of our tragedies is that we listen too partially and too briefly, and so the restlessness wears thin and the crying dies and the movement ceases. In the Emergence myth it is different. Now the existent ones, out of their tension, begin to make things. The four-story house at the center is not merely there; it is *put* there, firmly grounded in the lowest part of the darkness. Then, says the myth, they moved upward from the first to the second chamber: they moved upward "just because."

Is this simple statement, containing no reason within itself, merely a bad line from a poorly written tale whose author has not bothered to find the answer to "why"? Indeed it is not. Only our arrogance, the other side of our greatness, convinces us that "just because" is no reason at all. In truth, "just because" is the symbol for the ancient curtain of mystery hanging between us and all that we do not yet comprehend. How often we say "just because" when we do not know why we do what we do. Thus, sometimes "because" is the most that can be said of the strange first thrusts toward a fuller awareness, a more expanded horizon of consciousness.

And "they moved upward." This is the urge out of the restless movement in the surrounding dark. This is a first irrational kind of choice. So it must have been with the first creatures who forsook the comfort of the sea and moved upward onto land. They made a choice in favor of change. Should this seem fanciful, one must remember that what we know is very small compared to what we do not know. Maeterlinck said half a century ago:

> It comes to pass with the bees as with most of the things in this world; we remark some few of their habits; we say they do this, they work in such and such a fashion, their queens are born thus, their workers are virgin, they swarm at a certain time. And then we imagine we know them, and ask nothing more. . . . But let the eye draw near, and endeavor to see; and at once the least phenomenon of all becomes overpoweringly complex; we are confronted by the enigma of intellect, of destiny, will, aim, means, causes; the incomprehensible organization of the most insignificant act of life.[24]

There may not be consciousness as we know it in these first choices. But somehow some dim sense of meaning in nature, some irritable impulse in the apparently direction-less matter of the personality, forms a nucleus for an upward thrust. We do not know who or what makes the decision, or precisely when, but it is made. Choice seems to be there from the beginning. Who chooses cannot be answered. But in both the outward and the inward world it happens thus. Something knows; yet it is knowledge without a subject. When a creator-god, such as those mentioned, is present the choice is more clearly formulated. Even when a creator-god is not there, however, as in this Navaho Emergence myth, choices are made. For the creator-god also is at bottom a symbol of man's will to live.

An example of a combination of these two ideas—the "uncreated" will toward growth and the "creator" as a more sentient core of determination—is found in one version of the Zuñi origin myth: "Awonawilona conceived within himself and thought outward in space, whereby mists of increase, steams potent of growth, were evolved and uplifted." [25] Allfather (also Smiter, All-Knowing, Far-spoken, Shaker, Burner, to give a few of his names) was the Norse deity "there from the beginning of time," [26] a sort of presence standing for the idea of arousal to life. And the indeterminateness of even the "creator"-will is shown by the Winnebago words about Earthmaker: "Our father, on what must he have been sitting [when] he came to consciousness? Then his tears flowed [and] he wept. Not long did he think, not anything did he see, not anything was there anywhere." [27]

Wisdom and Knowledge first belonged to the animals, said the Pawnee Indians,[28] for Tirawa, the creator-god, "did not speak directly to man." Radin has written that a great many of the North American Indian tribes and clans believed in "one principle and several subordinate spirits in everything"; also he points out that dual "transformers" are found in "all parts of America." [29] Here again is the sense of a nucleus or center from which growth moves outward, with the "transformers" bringing to life what is present in the dark beginnings.

These same symbolizations can be seen in the cosmogonies of Africa, where the Shilluk and the Ashantis both describe a central "creator spirit" or being who either reflects himself in a many-faceted multiplicity of refractions (Shilluk), or manifests his power through a pantheon of gods, spirits, ancestors (Ashanti). For the latter, a god is "a servant acting as intermediary between creator and creature." [30]

The Dogon of Africa, referred to earlier, have a complex and remarkably profound concept regarding the "uncreated" and the creator. They have no creator-god as such. The "egg" of the world seems to be a given, containing the organization of the cosmos, of society, of the individual. This egg or seed breaks open, and a creative process begins.

All these images seem to relate to an effort of discovery, an attempt to apprehend the infinitely small at its point of departure towards the immeasurably vast. In fact, the order of the heavens, as it is observed and conceived by the Dogon, is no more than a projection, infinitely expanded, of events and phenomena which occur in the infinitely small. . . .

. . . but from the moment when beings became conscious of themselves and capable of purposive action, the course of creation developed, in Dogon thought, in a less simple fashion. Personalities appeared who, after the chief person, the Creator God *Amma*, moved in a world of feeling, resembling man's ideas of himself and his own activities.[31]

These mythic statements of the nature of whatever lies at the heart of life, at the beginning, point the direction of our apparently unwitting choice to evolve. The "infinitely small," the egg, the seed, the insects, reach for fulfillment, without at first "knowing" why. Seen in the light of our blind desire for growth, this subjectless knowing about the direction of movement is beyond measure valuable, because the subject who knows is a late-comer in the history of any single individual life, even as it is in the history of the race. So to be aware that in our restlessness and our agitation lies a spontaneous and irrational start of emergence is to dignify rather than to degrade the tortured times of disquiet which are part of our humanness.

It is also to open ourselves to the possibility of being able to go from where we are and do not want to be to where we are not and grope toward. Even a minor choice born of the frustration of immobility is a start. Sometimes just to be able to say, "I am lost. I cannot find my way," is a step taken beyond confusion and paralysis. The very word "I" makes the difference. It is a major transition for the child when he can refer to himself as "I," thus setting himself apart from the environmental mass. It is a major transition from neurosis to health when an adult can say "I" instead of "they" when trying to understand the sources of his problems. This "I," as it grows in the child, or as it repre-

sents a healthy and conscious structuring of the adult
personality, is the *ego*. The entire psychic edifice is no
stronger than the ego which is its responsible core. What
the myths indicate must never be forgotten: that the ego
does not come in some cosmic eruption, but evolves through
each small pushing hurt of psychological movement.

To return to the Emergence story, the six kinds of ants
and three kinds of beetles move upward. They move from
the central place of the four-directional darkness, and a vertical rises from the horizontal flatness of origin. So a vertical
mandala is present as well as a horizontal one. It is possible
that verticality was the first noticeable difference between
higher apes and *Pithecanthropus erectus*. Surely here in the
myth the vertical is an effective symbol of evolution from
the horizontal darkness upward, as is the spiral direction
in the Dogon concept previously described. And whereas
before there were only four directions—north, south, east,
west—now there are five, because "up" is added.

The symbolic meaning of "five," like all profound
meanings, is a paradox. For a child sees his body as one,
and his arms and legs as four astounding extensions of himself in space; in fact, he often draws himself as a fivefold
creature. The hands of man, with their five flexible fingers,
are superb and sensitive organs of making and mending,
healing and destroying, loving and punishing—in short, of
his most divinely human aspects. Cushing relates that the
Zuñi say five things are necessary to man:

> The Sun, who is the Father of all.
> The Earth, who is the Mother of men.
> The water, who is the Grandfather.
> The fire, who is the Grandmother.
> Our brothers and sisters the Corn, and seeds of growing
> things.[32]

In a Father Berard Haile discussion of Navaho head and
face marks, he states that five sacred stones were used in the
original hogan.

(The MS reads that previously "he took out [of his pouch] a turquoise . . . face print in the shape of our present thumbnail, a white bead in the shape of our present index fingernail, an abalone like our middle fingernail, a jet like our fourth fingernail, a red stone like our little fingernail" . . .).[33]

Among the ancients, five was sacred to the God of Light, and the five-pointed star was a mythical symbol of perfection.

The fifth direction, then, is a representation of our creatureliness in all its manifold urges and contradictions. But it is also the distilled spirit of our most unearthly achievement at any given point of time: the *quinta essentia*. Five, for the Navaho, is not only an active number but also, in many ritual and mythic groupings, "seems to be a combination of four and one, four of these objects, persons, or times being of ordinary value but the fifth exhibiting extraordinary characteristics." [34] In this myth, at this early crucial moment of change, five is both creatureliness and quintessence, both blind urge and devoted choice. The insects have centered their restlessness, and thus focused on the quality of the growth of the unconscious in man.

Summary
MATERNAL SUBSTANCE

The beings explored the second chamber out to its edge and found it went nowhere. Then one beetle, called Pot Carrier, found he had forgotten his pots and had to go back to the first chamber to get them. While the second chamber was larger than the first, there were still no stones or vegetation, no days, no light. Then the first beings met two Locust People, and they all went up to the third chamber.

They soon found this was not fit to live in and wondered what to do. Locust tried to advise them as to a course of action. But the people resented one person doing this and felt that all should participate in the decision, so a council of chiefs was called. The chiefs made a choice, and they all moved upward to the fourth chamber.

THAT which impelled the first thrust away from flatness and quiescence, that early not-to-be-denied tension of life's nucleus, now sends a movement out from the center toward the periphery. In the first darkness a mid-point was added when it was lacking; a place was made where the feet could be firmly planted. In this second darkness, radii are added from center to circumference so that the feet may walk from here to there and back again.

In the unconscious depths of the individual, too, these things occur, and not just once. Each fresh excitement in the darkness of new growth and new beginning is a first cry after birth, a pure expression of life and energy which must go somewhere. And when the going begins, though neither why nor whence is known, there is a point of non-darkness which is like a fixed star for the compass of the soul. Then exploration can come, and the edges of the dark can be felt even when they cannot yet be seen. This visionless intuition that something lies beyond—even in the unseen places—is in fact the genesis of the religious sense of meaning. Not that it is at this stage a full-blown metaphysical or mystical assurance, for it is not. But suffering, even of an inarticulable and unrecognizable sort, has a strange aptitude for minor wisdom. It sends small shoots of courage out in new directions. For each of us every start is a pain, and if we are willing to feel our way out from it, we may touch unseen dimensions in ourselves which are very like miracles. "How is it," wrote a friend, "that when I keep my nerve in a time when I'm afraid of the next step, something comes along that helps me?" Meaning is born precisely when we persevere although no meaning is apparent. In essence this is a religious experience.

The first chamber of the First World was the place

of Mother-night-and-nature where all things were one and nothing clear. This first chamber was the great vessel where no differentiation exists, the womb holding the mass of fertilized seeds of fruitfulness. This mother container appears in many myths toward the beginning of things. Earth Mother is the oldest female deity in most Norse tales, although some say Night is older, and some even name the Dark Moon as mother of Night.[35] Greek myth has three major origin stories, each of which contains the mother source.[36] Tethys conceived and bore the watery children of Okeanos. In Orphic writings Night, a bird-goddess with black wings, conceived of the Wind and laid a silver egg in the lap of Darkness. Finally, as Hesiod told it, came Mother Gaia, Earth, bearer of nature and giants. Bayley says:

> The Ancients conceived a primeval and self-existent Mother of all Wisdom, who figures in Mythology as *Magna Mater*, the *Bona Dea*, the All-Mother of the Gods. . . .
>
> In Babylonian cosmogony the Deep or Depth was regarded as a symbol of Unfathomable Wisdom . . . [who] was said to swell in the depths of the illimitable ocean, and was termed "the Lady of the Abyss." . . . It [Abyss] means the profoundest depth, the primal chaos, the unfathomable and unsearchable deep. . . .[37]

The "Mother-of-all" concept existed in many American Indian groups also. These excerpts from California Indian myths give a picture less complex than those of Babylon or Greece:

> The world was made from seeds. . . . The seeds were the earth.[38]
>
> The Mother-of-All (Tabiya) lived at a lake. . . . She had no man but she must have gotten one some way because she was going to have some babies.[39]
>
> A mother came out there and called forth every different tribe and told it where to go. . . . The water there is black, and if one watches one can see all kinds of animals running around under the water.[40]

In one very real sense, Mother-night-and-nature is quite indifferent to the fate of the seeds she holds in her vastness and chaos. If they grow or do not grow, it is all the same to her. She engenders, she contains, but the lonely individuation of the seed is not her task. Something more, something greater, is needed for the work to progress. The first something, in the present myth, is restlessness. The second is remembrance and recognition: remembrance of the first point of nondarkness which gave possibility of meaning, and recognition of the need for containing the possibility in a more concrete form.

One small and humble beetle called Pot Carrier remembers that he has forgotten. By his return to the lowest chamber to get his pots, he brings up from the depths of the mother her fruitfulness separated into more discrete and usable amounts. One definite being, at least, is no longer himself contained in the mother. This is an event of no little importance in the evolving of individual consciousness. For when some small bit of excitement focuses itself enough in us to help us remember and recognize what must be done, helps us wrest from the chaotic darkness a sense of containment and understandable purpose, we are to that degree freed from the oblivion of the mother world.

Memory, whether recognition or recall, is our relationship to our past and to our own evolving structure. Not to remember, as in states of amnesia or psychosis, is a horror and shatters us to our core because not to remember is, from the viewpoint of consciousness, not to be, not to have identity. Child and animal, living in the mother substance of immediacy, do not need to remember much. We must. The whole continuity of our consciousness depends on our remembering. And as we remember and are responsible for our remembered fragments, we are confronted by time and destiny. "This concern with a world in transition," writes Henn, "the attempt to relate past and present, appears to be a continuing aspect of tragedy." [41] Remembering is the excitement of learning, the wondrous face of love, the nervous words spoken in the therapist's office, the knife of grief. It is neurotic when it becomes ensnared in self-pity. When it helps us or is used by us to relate us to our ongoing-ness, it is, in effect, prayer. In this sense, "the word" and "remembering" seem to be psychological cousins.

(In this Navaho myth each chamber in the ascent through the First World is named a Speech or Action. And in the *Popol Vuh* referred to earlier, the creator-gods not only speak "the word" in the primal darkness but also de-stroy some of the earliest preforms of man because they do not "remember.")

There is, in another version of the Navaho origin myth, a scene where First Man, after the people emerge from a lower world, says to First Woman, "We have forgotten something below, why didn't you remind me?" She shows him she has remembered and in turn accuses him of having forgotten something. Later she says, "I never forgot any-thing, after the hogan is built I shall take care of it, for I forget nothing." [42] Thus recall, recognition, memory, are related to the vital sacred "word," to the growth possibilities almost left behind in the mother-womb. On a much more cosmic level than that of Pot Carrier's remembering is the Babylonian account of Marduk slaying Tiamat, the mother-dragon, and making her severed halves into Heaven and Earth. [43] Yet both Marduk and Pot Carrier are proclaiming the start of a new order by their acts of pulling movements up from the heavy darkness. It is most interesting to note that the Egyptian Scarabeus (Beetle) was the symbol of self-existent Being. [44] Surely Pot Carrier Beetle is becoming self-existent at the moment when he carries his own pos-sessions.

Before the upward progression, the original beings meet some Locust People. So the great restlessness of the number three remains: Ants, Beetles, Locusts. In Navaho symbol-ism, four and multiples of four are the seemingly dominating numbers and would appear to be more related to stability and wholeness. Reichard states, "The rule is that blessing and divinity are represented by even numbers, evil and harm by odd." She also says that the War Ceremony takes three nights.[45] Although she feels that no final conclusions as to number meanings can be reached, it would seem that this present myth's early emphasis on three—nine original insects, three kinds of insects—does point toward an unstable equilibrium leading to movement. It is possible that the Locust People add a less earth-bound quality to the insect company. It is also possible that this new triad is more defined than the earlier one, both because of the Locusts' increased mobility and because a Beetle has made somewhat clearer the awareness of how development must go on.

The fourth element, different in kind from the triad of insects, is represented by the pots themselves. The people now "own" the mother, with Pot Carrier as the formulator of the experience. In the myth of Prometheus, and in other similar "fire theft" tales, the hero goes up in order to bring the feminine vessel down. That is to say, at certain levels of psychological and of cultural development, the heaviness of purely material existence must be altered by a leap into the realms of light, by an act of will which dares to wrest from the universe what the universe is reluctant to give. Sometimes from our collective lives we must literally "steal" time for ourselves, love for ourselves.

At other levels of development the growth of consciousness has to come from the lowest place, from the undifferentiated but fecund earth of nature. This is not "material existence" as such. It is *prima materia*, the vessel, the place of the sprouting seed, the germination. This symbol of the vessel was basic in alchemical treatises. Jung has written: "In alchemy the egg stands for the chaos apprehended by the artifex, the *prima materia* containing the captive world-soul. Out of the egg—symbolized by the round cooking-vessel—will rise the eagle or phoenix, the liberated soul." [46]

The entire movement of dipping down and bringing

up—as seen not only in Pot Carrier's return for his forgotten pots but also in each oblique upward step of the early
part of the myth—represents that in us which acts to set
the "captive world soul" free. For as soon as the germination place, the *prima materia*, the egg, is claimed by the
individual—that is, is seen in an individual way—insight
can come. (For example, in the third level of the First
World the beings begin to know that this place is "not fit
to live in.") If the earliest dark earth-vessel is the irrational
and elemental foreground of the infant's world, containing
the demanding visceral impulses, the biological needs which
continually remind every man of his material reality, then
to begin to be free is to begin to know that life cannot be
lived forever at this level.

Instinctive feelings, sharp to our eyes if we watch
children and animals, are very akin to basic likes and dis-
likes. To recognize that this place is "not fit to live in"
is to bring earthy wisdom into the atmosphere of the
visionary idea—wisdom which has been there from the
beginning, yet which must be over and again realized and
made manifest in the clumsy ways of growth. We cannot
survive by the visionary idea alone. We must painfully
build our growth on the day-to-day realness of ourselves,
neither being inert within the vessel nor outreaching the
place where we are. This finding of balance between vision
and earth-reality is different for men and women. A man
must deal with the feminine in himself (what Jung refers
to as "anima") by taking his feelings with him as he goes—
as Pot Carrier takes his pots. He must guard against the
neurotic manifestations of Mother-night-and-nature, such as
lethargy and unconsciousness, or hostilities thrown at all
"mothers." The woman, on the other hand, must try to
find a quietly alive relationship to her own feminine nature,
without becoming herself a devouring female.

So the people recognize that the incompleteness bred
of impoverishment is upon them. But when Locust gives
advice, he only offends them, and they demand a council of

chiefs. Locust (Cicada), judging from his role throughout
Navaho mythology, is a spirit power as contrasted with
earth powers, and it is Locust who later makes the world
ready for occupancy after the flood. Here, however, it
seems that concerted action of the emergent beings is the
appropriate thing, rather than what might have been a
too quick spiritual leap. It is as if Pot Carrier's action was
a necessary singularity for the possession of the vessel, but
now there is need for a plurality to make truly conscious
what was before merely contained. Only with an organizing of the insights can the next move be apparent.
For the first time choice comes through a subject: the
council of chiefs. They are the now needed leadership and
experience.

A backward look at the First World chambers shows
how the image and idea have evolved from the excitement
of the ants and beetles, through the development of sen-
sation and perception in the remembering and carrying up
of the pots, to the first organization of this formless world.
And the last turn of this first spiral includes an expanded
perception of what the first excitement meant, as well as
a sense of the potentials for a wider life.

And what does this mirror in the evolving of the personality? How can we relate to this expanding meaning?
Although we as individuals are but fragmentary parts of the
greater image (archetype) of Man which moves in us,
yet we must relate consciously to the larger prospect of
our personal self contained in the archetype. We must,
that is to say, come to see ourselves as microcosmically
included in the same spiral journey which the myth tells.
The stirrings of restless excitement in any one of us are
always in some way beginnings. If they are permitted to
move about, they lead to a vision of what it means to be
free, to a remembrance of our own uniqueness, to a willingness to go forward. For us to sense our own smaller
myth in this wise, as a parallel to the larger creation myth,
is our gift to life. And we thus become aware of the

direction of our excitements, we can also begin to know that in us are the elements for potential leadership, for a quiet consideration of why and whither—in short, for the recognition of the possibility of a working together of our parts which can give rise to our fuller personality.

Freedom, uniqueness, seem like small things to achieve, rather strange gifts to life. How rarely we feel free, however; how rarely we sense our own uniqueness. A small dog, stirred by some inner excitement, will turn from play or food and trot determinedly off on his unique business without a by-your-leave. A young child is not afraid to say, "A hole is to dig," [47] or to describe a pool of oily rain water in a gutter as a "drowned rainbow," or to walk naked before guests. The child is still unconsciously contained in his myth, while the dog has none. Thus both are free. Usually by the age of six to seven years, or almost certainly by the time of adolescence and early maturity, we have forsaken our uniqueness and lost our freedom. After some forty years of blind and sterile compliance to the collectivities of parents and job, a man dared to make a "monster," as he called it, out of clay. This simple act of faith in what came out of his own lower world was, for him, an affirmation of his uniqueness and the first step toward freedom. So we, too, must return to where we started and gather our parts together, letting our restlessness coalesce and lead us up the forgotten path.

Summary
EMERGING DIRECTIONS

The fourth chamber was larger, still dark, from here the Moving Up or Emergence begins. Present were nine beings: two First Men, two First Women, First Made Man, First Made Woman, First Boy, First Girl, Coyote. Also Fire God (Dark God) was present.

First Man's wealth—White Shell, Turquoise, Abalone,

Jet, and Red-White Stone—he placed at east, south, west, north, and center.

It becomes more apparent now that those faculties developed at the "lower" levels of creation lead slowly toward man. In this fourth chamber are nine beings, and Fire God (Black or Dark God). These beings—particularly the eight first named—are the archetypal forms or images —"archai" or eternal presences in the mind of man before he realizes what he is.

Before Man as Anthropos, that is to say, there are already pre-existent images of Man. Part of the greatness of man is his ability to anticipate and to envisage what his capacity may be, even before it is realized. He can conceive of Man as something to be worked toward. Some Navahos are aware of this archetypal level. For example, the informant of Father Berard Haile's original version of the Emergence said, of a particular ceremony, that the rite "which was held here was more holy, because it was actually performed, while in the lower world it was typical only of what was to take place here." [48] Also, as Alexander says, while there are some American Indian groups who recognize creators or procreators, "the usual conception is either of a preexistent sky world peopled with images of the beings of an earth world yet to come into being, or else of a kind of cosmic womb from which the First People were to have their origin." [49]

If this Emergence myth had a creator-god, he would have made these beings. For when, as was stated earlier, a beginning is with a creator-god, that beginning is in the spiritual aspect, as is true of the Genesis myth. The Navaho myth, however, starts in nature, with the spirit implied as a goal to be achieved. One kind of creation is upward from the body substance (Navaho), while the other kind is downward from abstractions of the spirit (Old Testament). Man cannot arise in one cosmic leap from scattered chaos to fullness of order. The upward movement comes but gradually, out of the development of the eternal presences into the wisdom of the generations.

In the best sense, the miracle of human life is contained in the traditions. The First Man, the "first ancestor," is the representative of this tradition, this living and dynamic heritage, which grows and builds in the individual and in the culture as a foundation on which the future can rest. First Man is the Gnostic Anthropos, primal Man, related to heaven and earth, above and below.[50] He undertakes the subduing and organizing of nature, since his own pattern of evolution is toward even greater consciousness. His drive toward individuation generally affects all lower animal drives and slowly changes them. He is related to the deeper Self, and because of this must contain all things, including evil.

According to Kluckhohn and Leighton, "most of The People believe that First Man created the universe."[51] They also say that First Man and First Woman "were transformed from two ears of white and yellow corn." This indicates that despite the myth as told—or perhaps beyond it in its manifest structure—there is among the Navahos a sense that the potential Self is there from the beginning.

The mythic motif of primal beings, usually primal pairs, is widespread and remarkably consistent from culture to culture. The Babylonian epic tells of the male Apsu, the fresh-water ocean, and the female Tiamat, the salt ocean and dragon of Chaos, as the primeval engenderers. After them come Lahmu and Lahamu, Ansar and Kisar, Anu and Ea.[52] The two first men, and an Anthropos from whom things are made, appear early in the Iranian-Persian myth.[53] Eight primal beings—four pairs—were present in the world before the creation, according to an Egyptian account. These pairs were called "abysmal forces" (Niu and Nut), "endless space" (Heh and Hehut), "darkness" (Kek and Kekut), and "sultry air" (Niu and Nit).[54] Above was Awonawilona, say the Zuñi, "the supreme life-giving bisexual power, who is referred to as He-She, the symbol and initiator of life, and life itself, pervading all space." Then there were Sun Father, Moon Mother, and a number of other male and female terrestrial and subterranean gods including Salt Woman, Earth Mother, Corn Father, Plumed Serpent.[55]

The Fon of Africa sometimes speak of a creator and a creator's assistant working together. Moreover, they tell of an androgynous deity who was progenitor of the dual creator, the primal pair. The idea of twin beings "expresses the equilibrium maintained between opposites,"[56] which, for the Fon, is the rhythm of life and the nature of the world. The Arunta of Australia split their sacred bull-roarers into two, each pair being male-female.[57] Pawnee Indian ideas are that all things in the world are two. "Man himself is two in everything. Two eyes, two ears, two nostrils, two hands, two feet—one for man and one for woman. Stand in the sunshine and behold how man is two —substance and shadow, body and spirit. Even so there are sun and moon, and in moonlight as in sunlight man is two, always two."[58]

Series of couples also mark the advent of creation or beginning in the *Popol Vuh*.[59] There are Creator and Maker (Tzacol and Betol), mother god and father god (Alom and Qaholom), female god of dawn and male god of night (Hunapu-Vuch and Hunapu-Utui), and several other pairs. The myth states: "Only the Creator, the Maker, Tepeu, Gucumatz, the Forefathers, were in the water surrounded by light."[60] Tepeu and Gucumatz (sovereign, and plumed serpent) work together with Huracan (great lightning, or flashes of lightning and thunder), the "Heart of Heaven," in a sort of semidivine reciprocal communication on the images and preforms of man. "Then comes the word. Tepeu and Gucumatz come together in the darkness, in the night, and Tepeu and Gucumatz talked together."[61] It is as if here "the word," the Heart of Heaven, were in essence the aspect of oneness, sudden insight, the present truth of meaning which lies behind the dual appearance of things. Tepeu and Gucumatz and the other twofold deities are representatives of the duality of man, which includes the dimmer, slower ways of recognition and discussion, as well as realization of the natural development of personality from the moving darkness. We could say that we but slowly come to know the thoughts we are already thinking, through our alternations between opposites in ourselves. Only with restlessness, meditation, struggle, does what is "natural" and single in any real sense become conscious.

It is well to pause and examine where this idea leads. To assume a "natural gradient" of the psyche (as Jung has done), or an essential truth which life works to fulfill, or a preordered world of collective forms and images and eternal presences is also to assume a universe in which the totality of man is not just a plaything of quixotic gods. It is rather to say that God's totality (or the fullness of the gods) is there as a divine ground on which natural gradients operate in the direction of wholeness and the complete realization of previsioned potentials. It is also to assume a universe wherein a truly cooperative community of man and the gods is essential for the fulfillment of both. To be sure, "meaning" has no meaning except as seen by man's consciousness; but the idea of pre-existent forms and natural growth gradients assumes the possibility of being able to discover meanings rather than to invent them. It seems quite clear that these great creation myths are thus precisely the telling of this coming of man into his own. With the shift and flux of cosmic interrelationships and dualities, the pulsing of the points of light in the darkness, the idea of man slowly takes on a shape and a three-dimensionality and becomes a part of the living tradition of the ancestors.

Present with these eight "twin" beings is Fire God, or Dark God. In Navaho ritual, this Dark God of Fire is one who generally does not offer help, but must be approached, asked, persuaded out of his remoteness. As Son of Fire, in the Wheelwright-Klah version of creation, he is the angry one who, by his fiery actions, forces the people ever upward.[62] It is important that Fire God is here with these other less clearly differentiated deities because his presence emphasizes that fire and intensity belong first to the gods. If we assume the roots of creative intensity to be of our *own* making, we rob them of their strength. For Fire God is dark light, heat, the engendering vision in the unconscious depths—and the individual, ever and always, can relate to this, but cannot own it. (It is said that one name for Dionysos meant Son of Fire.[63])

All those present here in this highest chamber of the first dark world of the beginnings are still, however, only nonpersonal images pointing toward man's personal becoming. Nowhere has the awkward essence of creatureliness quite emerged.

And now Coyote comes into existence—Coyote, the small wild dog of the North American plains. In Navaho myths, Coyote is a mischief-maker, having all the diverse qualities of animal and man. He is sly; he is a knave; he disobeys; he blunders. But he is very persistent, he is sometimes wise, and he achieves much. He plays over and again a vital role in Navaho and other American Indian myths.

Curtin, one of the early chroniclers of Indian myth, reported that Coyote figured prominently wherever he was found. "He is a tremendous glutton, boastful, talkative, cunning, exceptionally inclined to the other sex, full of curiosity, a liar, a trickster, deceiving most adroitly, and is deceived himself at times. He comes to grief frequently because of his passions and peculiar qualities." [64] These would seem to be negative characteristics of Coyote, which he most surely has as an aspect of his humanness. The Skagit Indians, however, relate that Coyote, Mink, and Otter were in on all the arguments and discussions when the Creator was planning the world, and one great totem pole, portraying the Skagit story of creation, shows the Creator and Transformer with a dog sitting at his right.[65]

For the Columbia River Indians, Coyote is the Changer who defeats monsters and makes the world ready for human beings.[66] Merriam describes the California Mewan Indian Coyote as a pre-existent creator, a "divinity of unknown and fabulous 'magic,' whose influence was always for good." [67] For other Indian groups Coyote was one of the early beings possessed of supernatural powers.[68]

There is a striking parallel between the role of Coyote and the roles of such similar animal gods as foxes, dogs, jackals. The fox in Europe and the jackal in Egypt were both held to be makers of tracks; Anubis, the jackal-headed Egyptian god, was a pathfinder. In India, the dog Samama symbolized dawn.[69] Thus for thousands of years doglike deities have stood for wiliness, wisdom, cunning, deception, direction. They have been sniffers of the way, guardians, pathfinders, watchers, heralds, companions, intelligent seeers.

The appearance of Coyote in the Navaho myth is the time of the first personal emergence, thus the time of the scolder, the herald, the scoundrel, the disturber. Contained in this development is a profoundly great idea. At such a moment, when we first begin to sense the realities behind the images of our own possibilities, we are no longer contained in the unconscious semidarkness of the early mother-womb. Nor are we upheld by the confidence which accrued to us at the Pot Carrier level, when we were able to possess somewhat the sense of boundaries. We stand now alone, in the tragicomic state of self-recognition. And our innocence is gone; our original undifferentiated wholeness is taken away. Coyote is the perception of this and the disturbance resulting from this realization. Such a disturbance and loss of innocence are seen in the child's first departure from home to school, where he is plummeted into an essentially nonmothering world. In our adult life, Coyote is many things and appears often. He is the disturbing sense that we cannot stay where we are any longer. He is the herald of consciousness of our role in the world. He is the scolding and irritating awareness that we can no more retreat into the comfort of blaming "them" for our fate, that we must now begin to take responsibility for our own sins. He is the blundering and gauche way in which we must inevitably fumble our growth.

The entrance of Coyote into the orderly sequence of creation is paralleled in various ways in other myths. For example, the confrontation of Adam and Eve by the serpent, thus by their own divine-creaturely nature, left them less innocent and more challenged by the perplexities of growth. They were a step more distant from the Lord God and a step closer to the godlikeness of man. This roguish, unpredictable, and incomplete but wise self-potential is always recognizable at a certain stage of emergence of consciousness. As a Trickster figure—such as Coyote—it retains for some time the paradoxical qualities of man's full reality, although in some myths it later splits into two parts, one part being light, or good, or human, one part being dark, or bad, or animal.

In the Winnebago myth, for example, there are four figures who participate in the creation: one who wanders about and accomplishes nothing, one who fights with everybody, one who merely multiplies himself, and one who helps man.[70] All of these together become a cosmic trickster-hero. He may be portrayed as a man, a hare, a coyote, a raven, a naïve baby, a clown, but, as Radin points out in *The Trickster*, basically "he possesses no well-defined and fixed form."[71] This ambivalent animal-human, serious-comic aspect of the psyche is represented in the *Popol Vuh* partly by the giant Vucub-Caquix who tricks and is tricked, and later by artisan twins who are turned into monkeys and clowns. In this latter case the twins become the shadow of creativeness, the Trickster aspect of the saviour, which cannot ever rule but can be very vital when ritually circumscribed and kept in its proper place. Both Krishna (Hindu) and the Irish Ulster Cycle hero began as mischievous and tricky children.

Radin, discussing the old Winnebago view of the Trickster cycle, writes:

> The implication that, despite the fact that what would
> have been sins if we committed them, were not sins in
> Trickster's case because of the fundamental function he
> performed for man, is the essence of the old view. He
> symbolized the reality of things. One does not make judg-
> ments about reality.[72]

Also Radin believes that Trickster figures can be understood
only when viewed psychologically "as an attempt by man
to solve his problems inward and outward." [73] In this connection, Jung feels that a Trickster does mark a beginning
of true consciousness, even though the Trickster is awkward and dishonest and a fool. Perhaps even in the often
cruel tricks and laughter of children and fools, he believes,
there may at least be an awareness of values in the testing
of reality. As a culture or an individual develops a higher
consciousness beyond the early Trickster level, the Trickster may fall into the unconscious world and may thus
become a shadow figure lurking behind the achieved consciousness—as eventually the snake does in the Genesis
story.

With the coming of Coyote into the Navaho Emergence, protest and scolding and dissatisfaction are born
because the reality of being human is more taxing than the
innocence of being animal. The original vague restlessness
and irritation of the ants is more focused in Coyote. When
we begin to have even a dim idea of what we are, human life
is recognized as a "disorder." We then fall into a world of
disturbance and protest as we reluctantly wrestle with our
own meaning.

For it is easier—less painful, at least—not to have
meaning than to have meaning. The neurosis cries out,
"They are to blame!" or "I don't want to grow up!" or "If
only things had been different!" Neurotic order dies hard,
resists most bitterly the command to renounce simulated

perfection in favor of the disorder of being real. But the sign of impending change from neurotic enslavement to a freer reality is the acceptance of limitation, imperfection, awkwardness, as conditions of healthy growth.

Dreams very often are the vehicles for the transporting of our Coyote and our creatureliness from the unconscious realm into a world of conscious confrontation. This is known not only to modern depth psychology but to many "primitive" groups also. For example, the Arunta of Australia consider dreams as magic of great potency,[74] while Bunzel reports, of the Zuñi Indians: "Dreams are believed to be of supernatural causation, and foretell the future if one can properly interpret them. Certain persons in particular are believed to 'dream true.' "[75] When dream illustrations are given in this book, it is because they demonstrate what it means thus to "dream true" in one's own evolution. For example, a woman who had tried for thirty years to be "right" and "good" and had, nonetheless, come to a place where her anxiety and restlessness were more than she could bear, reported this dream:

> I was in a basement room, dark, empty. I climbed up a narrow spiral stairway. At the top was a trap door and I had to squeeze through it painfully. I found myself on a stage where a play was going on. I didn't know what play, or what my lines were, but I knew I had to go ahead and respond, no matter how awkward or embarrassed I felt.

Here is the disturbance and disorder of being real. Here is the blundering forward thrust of the maker of tracks in the desert, the Trickster, Coyote.

To go back to the myth, there are in this fourth chamber of the First World, Dark God or Fire God, then eight beings, then Coyote. Dark God, as we have seen, really stands apart as an impersonal unit of nonmoving illumination. This leaves the eight plus one, or the four pairs plus one.[76] That is to say, Coyote goes beyond the series of couples, beyond the series of doublings which represent the ambiguousness of the emerging light/dark, male/female, good/evil, and so on. And as Coyote goes beyond the rounded order of things, marked and basic changes occur in the myth. With changed structure and more dynamic content, the myth is ready to move from First World to Second World, and one end can become another beginning in the cosmic spiral movement after the actual setting in of the creative process.

What is the marvelous movement of this transition? Here begins the up-and-down, to-and-fro pulsating of action so characteristic of our Navaho myths. The horizontal is carried by the four directions, east, south, west, north. The vertical is carried by the ebb and flow of cloud columns, to be discussed in the next chapter. And between these two—the rising and falling, the extension—the drama of creation is begun in more light than marked the beginning. With the defined work of First Man, a creator is present. The male principle has risen above the darkness of the mother—a process which began with Pot Carrier's remembering and continues here in First Man's placing of his wealth at the four compass points. With a certain implicit but emphatic meaning, the god is now brooding over the abyss. And the "abyss" is now not only a movement but a moment, a directional space set in the rhythm of time. In striving to know ourselves, we must relate to the complete idea of ourself as a possibility. We must also, however, relate to ourself as a point in space and a span of time.

In Navaho cloud columns and their color symbolism as well as in direction symbolism, both the rich possibility and the bounded actuality are dealt with. The more prevailing color sequence is as it is seen here: white, blue, yellow, black. Each color marks not only a place but also a meaning and a treasure for that place.[77] White belongs to the east, to the dawn, and, in some instances, also to the moon. It has the cool and virginal character of the early softness of breezes before day comes. White shell is its jewel, and its meaning is purification. Blue is the color of the south and belongs to daylight and the sun's fullness. One feels, however, not a masculine sun so much as a warm, fructifying, feminine spirit. Its jewel is turquoise, and its sacred meaning is good fortune and the fertility of the earth. The feminine character of both white and blue is emphasized by the fact that probably the most divine member of the Navaho pantheon is Changing Woman, whose jewel is turquoise and who, in those myths where she is dual, is Turquoise Woman and White Shell Woman. The Egyptian goddess was known as Lady of the Turquoise,[78] and there is a close connection between east, Easter, dawn, and Ishtar, the ancient goddess "who descended to and arose from the underworld."[79] Both Tibetan and Finno-Urgrik tradition agree with this color symbolism—the Tibetan seeing east as white with silver jewels, the place of tranquillity, and south as blue with jasper, the place of riches and planting. For the Finno-Urgrik people the east is the place of silver sand, the south the place of blue jewel sand. Lamaism also puts white in the east and blue in the south.

Yellow belongs to the west and to the sunset, for the Navaho. Abalone is its jewel. Its meaning is sustenance. It has the feeling of an ending which is yet sustaining, of the work of the day brought to fullness, of the poignant joy of a closing. It is "a color of spiritual blessing and also immediate physical well being." It is also related to pollen.[80] Black is the north's color (except in those myths where east and north are reversed in color for religious reasons). It is night and darkness, the unknown. Its jewel is jet. And its meaning, contrary to what one stereotypically associates with black, is that of both origin and summary. Chinese symbolism carries out this idea by making north the place of yin; it is watery, is related to winter, to the dark warrior, the black tortoise. And interestingly enough, while north in Chinese symbolism has this somewhat negative meaning, it is also the place of peace. The Fon of Africa[81] consider black as related to night and the earth gods. Bayley says of black that it is a "symbol of 'the Divine Dark,' of Inscrutability, of Silence, and of Eternity."[82] Yellow and black are generally more masculine colors for the Navaho. And black is related to one of the great Navaho hero-twins, Monster Slayer.

Insofar as these colors mark place, space, and specific values, they are closely allied to age-old ways man has used to delineate meanings. Jung has dealt at length with the psychological significance of the ancient art of alchemy.[83] Color symbolism was always vital in alchemical treatises, and the classical colors, representing stages in the alchemical "work," were black, white, yellow, and red, in that order. The quaternity represented by the four alchemical colors is, says Jung, a sort of "preliminary stage" of the alchemical work.[84] Each color then comes to symbolize a further stage in the work of finding the Stone (Self). In a similar way colors are used in Navaho myth. Blackening, or the *nigredo,* the beginning stage of the alchemical-psychological process, is equivalent to the Navaho beginning world from which the forward progression began. These cardinal colors, directions, jewels, as handled by First Man, are then the enfolding and bounding of the cosmos over which the creator is laboring. They are time and eternity, feminine and masculine, cool and warm, light and darkness. They are a framework within which man may, sometime, operate.

Summary
DARKNESS AND DANGER

First Man breathed on the sacred jewels which he had placed north, south, east, west, and center, and five cloud columns arose and met overhead, and midday and night began. Coyote visited each column of light and "changed his color to match theirs. In this manner Coyote increased in importance with the nine peoples of this world. His power increased as he absorbed these different colors." Baskets of the holy jewels were at each compass point, with a basket of evil diseases in the center where the Red-White Stone and the many-colored columns were.

First Man and his companions, and Spider Ant, were all evil. The other Ant People were not.

The columns descended into the baskets, with the central column black at the bottom. Coyote explained the secrets to Spider Ant. Ant People then asked how they could proceed upward. Acting on First Man's instructions, and led by him and Coyote, all the people grasped the middle column which raised them to the Second (Red) World. All the evils were taken along. And before they left, First Man rolled up the four columns and tucked them into his pocket.

WHEN the people arrive in this topmost place of the First World, there still is no light from any sort of fire, despite the previous actions and considerations of the people. What is necessary, it seems, is that the creator put himself into the creation. First Man takes his four precious jewels in four baskets, places a basket at each of the four directions, and breathes upon them—as in Zuñi myth it is told that with "the breath from his heart Awonawilona created clouds and the great waters of the world." [85] In this breath, in this spirit given from the inward longing, is the creative act which reveals the inherent pattern and rhythm of existence. The cloud columns rise and meet and join to become Day and Night. From the baskets, feminine as the pots of Pot Carrier but softer, the columns emerge as phallic symbols.

The Fon of Dahomey[86] tell a similar story of a god setting up four iron pillars at the four cardinal points to support the sky. He puts coils around these—coils which relate to movement. In this African myth the god has dual aspects, male and female, which dual nature is indicated by the pillars upheld by the moving coils. In the Navaho myth, breath combines with columns, columns rise from baskets; thus here, too, the image of the divine couple, first seen in the earlier twinnings, now becomes a more real conjunction of male-female. First Man, by the act of breathing-upon, gives the "idea" substance. An outstanding element of nature is born when midday and night are set apart, and sleeping and waking belong to man.

When Coyote visits these four columns, changing his color to match theirs and increasing his power as he absorbs their colors, something more conscious is added to the process of time. If First Man actualizes, Coyote realizes the meaning of creation. His paradoxically divine absurdity gives him exactly the qualities needed for absorbing the sacred colors. His divine aspect lets him recognize and also desire the fullness of the unfolding cloud columns, while his absurdity keeps him related to the human and material roots of unfoldment. Coyote here, as elsewhere in the Navaho myth, is a wanderer, a changeling, one who does not quite belong. Precisely because he is the different one, the scolder, the outsider, can he be the realizer. It is psychological truth of profound import that only the outsider can become the insider, that only the foreign element can serve as the reconciler and helper. The "flash of insight" comes, time and again, at a moment when the familiar and acceptable solutions have been put by, because the known, the usual, has lost a freshness of vision and become static and commonplace.

The notion of some relationship between the "fool" and the god-realm is a most ancient one. Langdon has indicated that Bel-Marduk of Assyrian legend is related to the god Lillu, whose name means "feeble one" or fool. Lillu is related to Tammuz and to Gilgamesh. These Assyrian nature gods who are confined for a time beneath the earth seem to be related to "the fool," Langdon believes, and are connected also with the Sacaea festival marked by bogus kings and orgiastic celebrations.[87] Coyote, earthy even if not chthonic, is a mixture of authority and lasciviousness, of hero and ineffectual fool. Although extremely archaic by comparison and on an utterly different level, the

Navaho myth also seems to have a kinship to the Parsifal legend. The Grail hall and the Grail itself could come to a new fullness of light and life, it was said, only through the intervention of a "guileless fool." So came Parsifal, riding from his home seated backward on a miserable nag, dressed in tattered clothes, behaving in oafish awkwardness. He, like Coyote, was a half-divine and very human outsider who became the insider. The Acoma Indians, a Pueblo group, have a creation myth, one of whose leading characters is Koshari, clown, fool, blunderer.[88] He was, says the myth, "kind of crazy; he was active, picking around, talking nonsense, talking backward." When Koshari unexpectedly hatches out of an egg, he cries "Why have I come alive? Am I wanted?" Then he proves to be of great assistance to the shaman in the sacred rites.

Are not all these fools, clowns, tricksters, blunderers, in reality a part of redemption, or wholeness? Are they not, Lillu, Koshari and Coyote, Parsifal, the eager hope—sometimes childish, sometimes childlike—that the world is full of wonders to be explored? Sometimes their redemptive grace is recognizable in laughter and the comic touch and is manifested simply in our willingness to accept our errors and awkwardness and to chuckle with the gods at ourselves.

This whole creation is becoming not only a structure but a process exemplified by the circumambulation of Coyote. With the advent of Night and Day and the new realization of creation, the process becomes an unfolding and an infolding, a rhythm, the systole and diastole of life. The cosmic wholeness now begins to breathe. A mysterious and evocative richness is carried by the imagery of the cloud columns as they rise, pulsate, fall, and are rolled into small spheres to be tucked into the pockets of First Man. What a greatness in so minute a space!

This cloudlike nature of the columns is not unlike the Greek development of *ideas*, found most clearly in Plato's *eidos*,[89] and it shows the Navaho myths as capable of genuine abstraction in thought. All mythic systems have implicit or explicit philosophies permeating them. For some, matter is primary, while for others the idea comes first. In this part of the Navaho myth the image as an idea is basic. A cloud has no substance, but it conveys the image of substance. What is preserved in a heavenly place, one can never have. But its equivalent can, like clouds rolled up in one's pockets, be possessed, and can then be pulled out when a need is there. So the dawn of ideas, in myth as in the striving consciousness of man, must give rise to endless recreations and cycles of change to make the ideas real. First Man and First Woman, First Made Man and First Made Woman, and the other early couples are all ideas and images of man and the creative process. And Coyote, Child of Dawn, of Sky Blue, of Twilight, of Darkness, is the outsider, the transformer, the realizer of the idea in fact.

What does this point to in the individual human psyche —this notion that idea must be realized *in fact?* No genuine psychological growth occurs until and unless the rich inner values and potentials of the unconscious strata are actualized—that is to say, are lived in the homeliness of every day. There is a second sin which is equal to the first sin of being cut off from the unconscious world. The second is the sin of being so enchanted with the inner images and archetypes that one becomes a curator rather than a creative experiencer. The great pulsating archetypes —like Shadow, Mother, Father, Self, and the others—rise and fall, expand and contract as columns of light. But unless our Coyote side takes them into the imperfect daily round of existence, walks with them to the table, the workbench, the relationship, they sink back into the baskets and never have real meaning. It is unfortunately not as taxing to talk about—even to see in operation—the archetypal major darknesses as it is to admit to the humiliating effects of our personal, dark and hidden side. Indeed, the archetype of suprapersonal Shadow has a certain drama about it, making it in a strange way more permissible. It is not uncommon for a person to retreat from the responsibility for bad human relationships by saying, as I heard one woman say, "But my Shadow is so big and terrifying! People should understand that! I can't do anything about it." This was not the cry of a terrified psychotic, but the infantile demand of an egocentric woman who would not face her own irritating little meannesses.

One suddenly sees, startled, that evil comes here in the First World, in the beginning world, as if evil were as natural as good. It is mentioned almost casually, at the same moment the cloud columns are seen in all their fullness. The central basket is filled with evil diseases. First Man and his companions, and Spider Ant, are evil and are practicers of witchcraft. And the Ant People are naïve and do not know these things. According to Goddard's version of the creation the "yellow jackets and black ants in the first and second worlds had stings with which they bewitched people." [90] That the insects were both good and evil is evident in the fact that Red Ant Way is under Holy Way, and Red Ant Evil Way is under Evil Way.[91]

For the Winnebago, too, evil was present very early. After Earthmaker had completed the creation, he heard the people crying. "What is the matter, how can that be?" he wondered. "I imagined that I had created them with a sufficiency of life." And when he looked down, he saw that evil spirits from above, below, and on earth were working on man.[92]

One wonders why, at this time of first fullness, evil is so sharply present. There is not a single and simple answer, for the problem of evil is not a simple and single one. First of all, in a certain sense evil is a natural and early element in human life. For primitives and for children the forces of natural existence are cruel, hard, ruthless, unpredictable, and thus evil. These are fundamental facts and must be dealt with.

The second answer is more subtle. In the myth, evil is in a magical form, related to witchcraft. It must be kept in mind that psychologically there are two forms of "magic": black magic, used for the furthering of *personal* power and domination, and white magic, used more *impersonally* for healing. In both cases, mysterious resources and "mana" are involved, but differently harnessed. Egocentricity, arrogance, inflation, the desire for infantile omnipotence—in short, all the various defensive bulwarks built against insecurity—lead to the use of creative forces in the psyche for personal power. This use, which is really misuse, is "black magic." Possession by or identification with some impersonal and cosmic archetype often gives us tremendous power, enabling us to become "black magicians"—Rasputins, demagogic rabble-rousers, Hitlers. The true leader or healer, whether a tribal shaman or a Gandhi, is in the opposite sense a "white magician," impersonally offering his creativity in the service of his particular stratum of the human family.

Among the Abaluyia of Africa, rain was controlled by magic and magicians and not by political or priestly authorities. Diviners and sorcerers are believed to "own" their art.

> It is ours since a long time ago:
> We have bought it from no one,
> It is ours.
> It came with us from the Lake;
> With us, the uncircumcised ones of the Lake.[93]

This is certainly a dramatic example of "white" magic.

Reichard points toward what the evil could mean when she states, "Eliminating the fact of sorcery and the struggle to overcome it is like treating the Old Testament without sin." [94] And she continues: "Thus evil is the same as ignorance. . . . This means then that sin as conceived by the Navaho is not a sense of personal shortcoming influenced by consciousness and will, but either lack of knowledge of the proper order, or possession of that knowledge and its use for evil purposes."

When Navaho myth calls witchcraft evil, as it does at this point, and witchcraft is connected with magic, thus implying "black" magic, a moral point of view is taken. It seems psychologically sound to assume that this use of "evil" is in reference to what *appears evil in retrospect*. The tellers of the myth, the medicine men or priests, could see what the dangers of growth were. In the same way among us those who work at consciousness soon learn how negation and affirmation walk hand in hand, how forward and backward are necessary polarities for evolution. And so "evil" is as intrinsic in the upward progression as any other element. This is why "above" and "below" are equally sacred in Navaho mythology. Perhaps one clue to this is found in the ambiguous statement of First Man in a later episode of the Navaho Emergence. There First Man, accused of being evil, replies, "It is true, my children, I am filled with evil. But I know when to use it and when to withhold it."

Zuñi myth relates that two lost beings seen to come forth from the underworlds were witches, man and wife, "who were all-powerful for good or evil." [95] These witches demanded a human sacrifice so that rain could come and crops grow. In neither Navaho nor Zuñi examples is witchcraft *necessarily* black magic. Choice is possible as to the manner in which power is utilized. In this connection a superb Shilluk proverb says that "God threads good and evil men on a single string";[96] and the people of Ruanda hold that their dominant, powerful, and good god Imana "does not cause any evil but he allows the causes of evil to act." [97] The good or the evil is thus placed under the aegis of individual decision, is made a condition of personal responsibility. Blunders are only "evil" in the ultimate sense, it would seem, if they become dogmatic.

So the final movements in the First World are filled with paradoxes. The central basket holds both the Red-White Stone and diseases. The central column arising from this basket has, as its base, black as the medicine against evil.

The nine beings use the Holy Stones for food, and yet they practice witchcraft. First Man, although a possessor of evil, directs the upward movement by way of pillars of light and prayers in the different directions. He is also the carrier of the rolled-up cloud columns. And when the people enter the Second World, they bring not only the pillars of light but also all the evils contained in the central column on which they had come, the column resting on the Red-White Stone.

Red is sometimes a sinister color for the Navaho, related to danger, war, sorcery,[98] and is often paired with black. It is also a color of power and vitality.[99] Here the strange red-white combination gives a feeling of the danger of the new rather than of evil. It is, in fact, the Red-White Stone which affords the clue to this amazing play of opposites. Movement is, psychologically speaking, a dangerous thing. So long as the creature is quiet, passive, static, there is less chance of detection and confrontation and threat. The small animal, freezing into immobility in the face of possible danger, knows this. Yet no movement means no growth. Even the tree, motionless and quiescent in its winter silence, stands guard above a voiceless activity underground and inside its living fibers, and root and sap are far from static. When this busy changing bursts into bud, however, danger is there at the moment of birth—danger of frost, danger of blight, danger of drought.

And so it is, perhaps, with all living things. The Red-White Stone is there at the center and heart of being, and every new thrust is a new dawn and a new danger. A shy child put suddenly into an unfamiliar situation often shrinks away, hides itself behind its hands, or its mother, or some inanimate object. It is not necessarily wrong in this, for its ego may be so weak as to need protection until it is ready to emerge. There is a true danger for the very young and weak within each of us—a danger that if they emerge too soon, or at an inauspicious moment, they may be devoured by the fearful father of conformity.

The essence of this series of contradictions is that man must, as Kierkegaard said, breathe in necessity and breathe out possibility. To the extent that light comes, the whole darkness of life is seen. Yet it is usually brutal, even seemingly evil and dark necessity which drives man toward the larger possibility—as it drives the people in the myth. Whenever we reject the inspiration of necessity, or try to forsake the evil in our own baskets, we become more feeble as personalities and less able to expand into our potentialities. If we cannot admit that we err, that we are imperfect and unlovable and petty, surely we will never see ourselves as we are and will never even approximate completeness. A reason why projection—putting outside what belongs inside the psyche—is so disastrous is that it makes us flat, two-dimensional, and quite successfully prevents self-realization. One woman with whom I had worked long and patiently, trying to help her to recognize how she was the cause for her lamented lack of friends, finally ended our relationship by informing me that it was my meanness and my dishonesty which kept her from growing. Subsequently the same pattern was followed with several other therapists, always with her final refusal to be conscious of her own imperfections.

Unconsciousness is really a sin against the possibility of being man, so consciousness of evil and of its place and power is essential for psychological "salvation." The role of Coyote points toward this, in his absorption of the sacred colors. Spider Ant, as a good-evil being, corresponds and relates on the more earthly plane to Coyote on the holy plane. Spider Ant gets his magic from the godlike beings and yet seems, like Coyote, a carrier of the mystery of the psyche which is both good and evil.

The Emergence journey is not only one of increasing the areas of light but also one of progress from nonhuman to warm-blooded creatures. This is precisely where Coyote and First Man play a most vital part. Coyote partakes of the power of all the cloud columns and makes this power a part of himself. First Man helps in the creation and carries in his own pockets the multicolored microcosm. In this way both of them share the holy language of song. And they can begin marketing, can enter into a practical exchange of goods by way of prayer and ritual. These "covenants" implicit in rites and prayers are exchanges between man and the gods. They are bargains. Bargaining is a very human trait and in one sense is the basis of all human relationship, sometimes for better and sometimes for worse. Bargaining climbs above the cold-blooded level of existence by demanding at least some degree of responsible cooperation from each party to the bargain. For example, a good marriage demands of each partner not only honesty about personal needs and shortcomings but also a willingness to compromise in many areas, an ability to cooperate in mutual enterprises where neither can have his way totally and where both are served meaningfully. (This, to be sure, is a "bargain" in a much different way than the barter of a neurotic for the attention of mother or father surrogates.)

The "divine bargain" is the establishment of a true contract between man and the gods, between man and the numinous inner world of suprapersonal images, whereby each party gives honestly to the other out of fullness as well as need. The "neurotic barter" is an attempt by man to make his partialness seem wholeness through psychological protective coloration, through trying to "win" the outward other or the gods or God by praise, self-condemnation, infallibility, hostility, and other masks of uncertainty. When the bargain is between the human and the godlike, it is often told in the occult ritual language which leads to a realization of wider meanings not present before. In *African Worlds* it is said that

> the Ashanti believe that every man receives a *sunsum* and also a *Kra*. A man's *sunsum* is his ego, his personality, his distinctive character. It is not divine, but perishes with the man. A man's *Kra* is a life force, "the small bit of the

Creator that lives in every person's body." It returns to the Creator when the person dies. It is the Supreme Being that directly gives to a man this spirit of life when he is about to be born, and with it the man's destiny.[100]

So the life forces push onward. So, with this human divine bargain carried in the pockets of First Man, with the changeableness of Coyote, with the secrets learned by Spider Ant, the people grasp the central column and are moved into the Second World. But they bring with them *every* thing from the First World: black and white, night and day, good and evil.

III

Conflict of Forces

Summary

WHENCE AND WHITHER

First Man brought the rolled-up columns from the First World. Sphinx Moth Man and Woman lived in this Second (Red) World, and they had light columns similar to First Man's. Nevertheless First Man placed his balls of bright columns at the cardinal points, with the dark ball in the north as a gift to Sphinx Moth Man, who then blew smoke at them, and they expanded and grew.

Sphinx Moth Man asked the people from whence they had come. Ant People told him and asked him what they should do now. He replied, "I am big, but not very wise and know not how to get at things." Four times they asked him. Finally they offered smoke to him. He blew smoke in all the various directions, and they moved upward into the next level of the Second World.

In the second level of the Second World, First Man caused his columns of light to rise overhead as he had before. He placed a perfect White Shell disk in the center to bring about movement there, but nothing moved. He tried Turquoise, Abalone, Jet, but still nothing moved.

Finally First Man placed the Red-White Stone in the center, and the earth shook. He said, "This portends evil. This is not good, children." The earth-shaking increased, and the people were afraid. Finally the Red-White Stone moved up and carried the people to the next level of this world.

THE Navaho First World is the dark world, where the beginnings are insectlike, nonhuman, dimly seen. Then the slow evolving begins, with new life forms appearing at each world. There is a considerable body of mythological material presenting similar worlds. Polynesians and other Oceanic groups conceive of creation as proceeding from level to level, from darkness to light. The Zuñi describe a series of worlds beginning with the "blackness-of-soot world" as the first, followed by "water moss world," "mud world," and then "wing world." "The undermost world," so the Zuñi myth goes, " was so dark that the people could not see one another." [1] Bunzel describes this as the "four womb caves" of Earth Mother, from which man emerged. She also indicates that the Zuñi word for womb literally means "inside space." [2] Curtin told, many years ago, of the various worlds of California Indian myth, with the first one being a "burning world," then "water" world, "rock" world, and our present earth.[3]

At least one African group,[4] the Banyarwanda, tell of three worlds or levels, one above and one below our own. Better known, of course, is the Norse myth which describes nine worlds or levels of existence, all held together or united by Yggdrasill, the World Ash, whose roots reach Asgard, Midgard, and Niflheim.[5] The Chinese *Book of Changes* refers again and again to the "above" and the "below." [6] In many Gnostic systems there are various levels of existence which include a world of darkness, intermediate worlds, and a world of light.

What is being suggested by these widespread mythic motifs? In a simple way, it is that life begins somewhere in the imperceptible reach of the unknown, is sensed, smelled out, felt—and from then on, with that first strange moment of awareness, life grows from germ to sprout. Whether the lowest world is explored by torchlight, as in Zuñi myth, or by insect antenna, as in Navaho myth, it is surely the world where ideas about, and images of, man are turned over dimly in the mind.

With the Second World, the Emergence myth begins to be more specific and more concrete; we find more precisely sketched out the complex interweavings of light/dark, day/night, good/evil. The foundation has been laid in the dark beginning world—a foundation which will persist throughout the various worlds. It is a ground of fourfoldness, of four directions, four sacred stones, four rooms, four worlds. This is a deep affirmation of the balanced nature of the psychic personality. It says, in effect, that in our basic structure we are related to an image or idea of wholeness. Upon us falls the responsibility of realizing and actualizing this in the long arduous way which is both our historical evolution and our personal development. We cannot do this at first from a conscious vantage point, for the ego as such is not ready for mature involvement. That which is not us—not in the later way of a ready sensibility and discrimination, at least—cannot fulfill the demand for functional wholeness. The "above" and the "below" can and do exert their magnetic attractions, however, and a beginning can be made.

First Man, the creator-being, is working at his task. But instead of the unfocused restlessness and irritability of the first scenes, soon there will be a direct conflict between him and the warm-blooded creatures of night, the Feline People. A clash of forces cannot be long held off when the above and the below build up unresolved charges of energy. Nonetheless the tempo of the myth slows at this crucial point; the conflict is suspended, as if there were a time needed for consideration of the *before*, lest the *after* rush in too abruptly.

First Man has brought with him the cloud columns, the miraculous pillars of light which marked the boundaries of the first dark world. They are in his keeping, in the small compass of seedlike balls. And his first act is to set them in their places. The growth potentials born of the first dark unknown are not forgotten. They are, as has been said, the microcosmic covenants, the media of exchange at each new step upward and outward. That these rolled-up columns are related to exchange and interchange is made clearer now, for it is not First Man who makes them rise. Their movement in this Second World comes with the breath of Sphinx Moth Man, a demigod belonging to the Second World. So the rhythmic inhale-exhale of the previsioned psyche does not stop; it is only that the area which breathes grows wider and deeper and ever more inclusive.

The *Popol Vuh*, while it does not describe creation by levels, does tell of several preforms of consciousness—"mud men," "stick men," and others—each one being in one way or another an expansion of what preceded.[7] The Frost Giants in Norse myth[8] were the first forms of life; they were killed, and earth was made from their carcasses. Then dwarfs grew "like maggots" in the carcasses, but "at a word of the gods they became conscious with the intelligence of men and had human form. They lived in the earth and rocks." In one version of the Acoma Indian myth, it is written:

> They came out of the earth, from Iatik, the mother. They came out through a hole in the north called Shipap. They crawled out like grasshoppers; their bodies were naked and soft. It was all dark; the sun had not yet risen. All of the little people had their eyes closed; they hadn't opened them yet.[9]

There is a clear deepening and widening of the scope of creation in the Zuñi myth, too, where the progression is from darkness to water moss, to mud, to wings.

If this growth upward, expansion outward of myth is a paradigm for man, it means that mere additive change is not in fact change at all. When we change, we not only add to our awarenesses but widen our area of responsibility and so are able to respond to a more comprehensive slice of existence. It is for this reason that, in the beginning of Second World, the character of Sphinx Moth appears.

First Man's light cannot rule the world, else ultimate Man would always be creature and never cooperator.

Who or what is this strange new divinity, Sphinx Moth Man (Tobacco Horn Worm Man)? To see either caterpillar or winged adult of the sphinx moth family is to understand. Truly here is a god in the small. The caterpillar, long as an index finger, is proud in his vivid green, marked segmentally with white or orange dots and white, yellow, or brown stripes or arrows. He often has a hornlike tail and will rear up in a warlike stance if molested. The adult moth, subtly colored, has a wingspread of three to four inches and is very like a hummingbird in the energy of his nectar seeking in the twilight hours. Sphinx Moth, the diminutive horned god, the mercurial little body of pulsating wings—it is he who activates the light columns carried and placed by First Man. He is the possessor of similar light columns carried in this Second World. But to have used his own would have been to cut off the flow of life from below upward, to keep autonomous what had already come into being.

Each division of diurnal time has its own light: dawn, high noon, sunset, moonlight, and starlight. A particular light belongs in the same way to every fresh vista opened to us in the individuation process. Yet we must always bring with us the central illumination of our original dedication lest the new light fade, or lead us astray. (Both the new light of Sphinx Moth and the old light of First Man had to be rooted in this place.) The care required in determining what light is to be followed, and from what source it emanates, is vividly demonstrated in the Gnostic legend about Sophia.[10] Sophia, in the intermediate realm of existence, longed for the higher realms. She saw a shaft of light which, unknown to her, had been placed by the god Arrogant (Ialdabaoth), and she assumed it would lead her upward. However, Ialdabaoth had cleverly deceived her by pointing his light downward, although it appeared otherwise, and Sophia found herself plunged into the lower realm of Chaos. In like manner, in the Old Testament story, Jonah, having fled God and then found God again during his entombment in the great fish, falls into the trap of his own arrogance and is angry with God for not rigidly adhering to His original threats.[11] And all too often we, swept away by a genuine achievement of consciousness, fail to remember where the light began, and fall into the slough of one-sidedness again. So Sphinx Moth had first to breathe on the original columns, to root them in this Second World, before his own light could legitimately arise.

What grave errors we make when, before we move on, we do not allow this vital interchange which is renewal. Temptation always lies in the too fast, too large leap into newness. The rolled-up balls of possibility found in the darkness are left behind, or are assumed to be complete and sufficient. Arrogance steps over the horned worm, the dimly seen moth. Thus the meaning of going with the gods is not understood, and the significance of the pauses for renewal of the *before* and rehearsal for the *after* is overlooked.

In one part of the Zuñi ritual, the narrator says: "Here we will sit perfectly still for days, which will be precious, and our hearts will speak with the gods of the inside water place; all wish to meet together." [12] Sphinx Moth forces this same nonactive action upon the emerging people by asking the question, "From whence did you come?" The Hypnerotomachia relates how the hero Poliphilo, fearful, weary, consumed by torturing thirst, yet anxious to be on his way, finally sinks down under a great tree to think about his wanderings and submit to his fate.[13] Over and again in myth this question is raised. And an answer must be given before the going on is possible.

Here the answer comes from the Ant People, the first beings from the lowest place of origin. Is this not very right? Surely one of the most basic values of renewal and rehearsal is the honest telling to ourselves of the places from which we came and the ways in which we came. The too often unacknowledged sources must answer. These restless, ill-defined, unaccountably busy urges and irritations and searchings must be the first to say from whence. By answering so, by feeling into the whys and the ways of our coming, we are preparing for the next confrontation by our destiny.

No one can go forward without these periodic pauses for self-examination; nothing is more valuable than the humility required for submission to the place and circumstance of the immediate moment. Why are we not getting any place, we ask impatiently. We have worked hard, tried everything, called on the unconscious for a great dream, or even for a little one. Nothing happens. We thirst, and we are afraid. Perhaps it is that we, like Poliphilo, have not submitted to our fate. We have not listened for the questions life is urgently asking. Time and again, in both Zuñi and Navaho myths, the words are spoken, "Who are you? Where did you come from? Why?"

Only after the answering comes the further asking. And not just one asking; four times the Ant People importune Sphinx Moth with "What now?" Their breath, their life force, their smoke, is given him. After remarking on his own lack of wisdom, he marks out the boundaries again, circumscribes their space in blown smoke. On the vertical breath the people go forward. It is as if an ephemeral chain were being forged—a chain of time and space and movement. The restlessness recognizes itself and records itself. The restlessness offers up its strength to the concealed god, the small one. He blows time and space into a larger thing. This vague response to "What now?"— vague and formless as rising smoke—is the only possible one. What-nows and Whithers are satisfied by the faces turned in a new direction and the feet moving forward.

The pell-mell forward rush of this modern world is exactly our curse. It thrusts us backward because it leaves us breathless—and we do not take time to breathe, to send the smoke into the corners of our inwardness and wrap it about with patient devotion. Is it possible that one of our most dire inheritances from the nineteenth century is the impatience of the Industrial Revolution? All things are possible to man, we said. And the sooner the better, we added, with enviable assurance. The effect of this has been to hurry our every action, to make us more concerned with where we are going than with where we are. A new model of ourselves is anticipated annually, along with the automobile, the dishwasher, the jet plane, the lunar module. Thus we leave ever further behind the "outmoded" primeval soul, to make its peace with God as best it can. "Who am I? And from whence have I come?" are questions for the most part treated as the aged are treated— with a slightly superior tolerance for their vagaries. It is no wonder, then, that modern man has to learn painfully the meanings of compassion, patience, and love. And not only between nations and peoples, but between "I and Thou." How are our splits to be healed, our restlessness appeased, except by time spent first in listening and then in answering? Each next step requires this of us before it can be taken.

After the necessary "stopping to think," the listening and the answering, movement can go forward. First Man, ancestor, creator, once more becomes a doer, and his "doing," as is so often true when the image of man is trying for consciousness, constellates tension. The inevitable consequence of renewal and rehearsal is a shaking up which is intrinsic to the learning of growth. Not by the gods alone is the idea of being man pushed into reality. Nor is the slow wisdom of ancestral evolution, pulling mightily toward fulfillment, enough. The vigorous germ of that which deeply desires to live must break through, with fear and pain, if the original dim "knowing" is to be more than just that. Thus First Man now seems to be not only the better-defined carrier of the nature of the earlier series of couples but also a kind of "arouser," a kind of primitive

thunder god with the Red-White Stone a minor thunder-
bolt.

In a version of the Navaho Feather Chant recorded by
Maud Oakes,[14] First Man, although less disturbing than
here, is quite clearly the image of humanness assisting in
the creation, while First Woman is the suprapersonal *prima
materia* possessing the divine substance for creation. In
the Oakes story, First Man, advised by First Woman, aids
in making the hogan and the rising mountains and then
says, "I will live by everything the mountain has, by that
I will multiply, I will walk on a pollen road, Pollen Boy
will go in front of me, and in back of me and under me.
His words will I speak, I will live like him, and no harm
will come to me." First Man is a less active co-creator in
the Oakes version and a more active protagonist in the
Haile-Wheelwright version. In the latter account used
here, the ever expanding and more clearly defined potential of wholeness must continue its growth, not in the ways
of perfection, but in the ways of turbulence. If First Man
is part of the effort of the culture to find a new form of
consciousness in an unorthodox shift toward a different
way of being, then upheaval cannot be avoided or post-
poned.

When old patterns and attitudes are being shattered,
and when their successors are not yet understood, it is as
if confusion penetrated all the land. One cannot always dis-
cern which way leads forward. "How can I know," asked
a perplexed young man, "whether what I want comes from
the reactionary me or from myself?" We may not always
know, but can only attend to the confusion, wait upon it,
and see what happens. In the myth at this point it is as
if the light columns were illuminations from the unknown
or unconscious side of things and had to be somewhat
stirred in an unfamiliar way. The still-not-quite-compre-
hended light from the dark beginning rises and falls,
rhythmically and impersonally. That, according to the
myth, seems not to be quite enough. Another kind of

movement is required: perhaps some dynamic of irregularity and unevenness to institute a break in the endless cycles of the unhumanized images.

No perfect instrument will serve. First Man tries a perfect White Shell disk, stone of the east and dawning. He tries thereafter, in turn, a Turquoise, stone of the south, of midday, Abalone, stone of the west and sunset, and Jet, stone of the north, of night. And nothing really moves. Only the lovely and pure columns stand in their appointed places, marking the place and structure of possibility, but not the pattern of alteration. The flawless balance of colors, directions, diurnal rhythms is but an endless wheel turning back on itself. If the individuals are to have meaning they must go ahead. For them to do so, the pristine quality of this moment must be broken.

It is then that First Man tries the Red-White Stone in the middle place—the same stone that, in the First World, lay in the center basket containing the evil diseases. If red, in Navaho symbolism, is a sinister color relating to the dangerous, and white is the color of awakening and purification, it is difficult to avoid the implication. To be able to move, to take the step into time and change and consciousness, is to put at the center the purifying element of danger. Reichard states that red "is the color of danger, war, and sorcery as well as their safeguards";[15] Newcomb says of red: "It is a color of fierce power" and "occupies an important place in the color symbolism of all Navaho sandpaintings, as it represents the life principle of animals and humans as well as immortals. It may also designate the symbol which causes death." [16] It is often used in the sandpaintings to indicate "the life and power within." These two authoritative comments further underline the value of the Red-White Stone as an arouser and, eventually, as a light bringer. When it was placed, the earth shook, and First Man said, "This portends evil. This is not good, children."

How is it that this is so? Why is the sacred stone which brings about the desired upward movement also that which violently disturbs the people and makes them afraid? How can we understand this paradox as it touches the problem of psychological development in mankind and in us as individual members of mankind?

If we are to achieve a place beyond where we are—beyond wherever we are at this moment of time—we must dare to risk ourselves. The difficult and the dangerous must be our moving substance. We must choose to use this substance, to let it serve us in its sacred and cleansing and arousing power. And this not only in the large matters, for that is strangely easier. Most particularly it is in the small daily courage of daring to be no more and no less than what we are. Deep are the shakings of our comfortable earth when we are willing to act thus. For we are relinquishing the state of unconsciousness, we are forsaking the immovable desired perfection. This portends evil; this is not good. That is to say, this leads into greater freedom of choice; alternatives are present; and a new darkness of our own making is for the first time possible. Heretofore the "evil" has been in creatures who could be vanquished and in the immortal Holy Ones by voluntary actions. Now it exists in the very uncertainty of the earth, in the very insecurity of the forward movement. At such a time we as individuals must assume the responsibility for that which shatters us, rather than pushing it onto some parent or demigod or life force apart from ourselves. It is *our* Red-White Stone, looked at from the experiential point of view, which *we* have put at the center of things to upset the quiet placidity. And it is *we* who are shaken by our own action. Thus we see that we are both he who places the stone of disturbance and those who are in fear and trembling. The loss of perfection and balance is the gain of the next stage of development. From the valley of our imperfection we can begin to walk on our own feet.

Summary
CLASH OR COOPERATION

The next chamber of Second World was the home of all the Feline People, who were tricksters and at war amongst themselves. The newcomers joined up with the various warring factions. First Man made some of the Felines his house guardians.

The Feline People tried to injure First Man, coming at him from each of the four directions. Each time, however, their arrows were deflected, and First Man killed a few of the enemies and revived them in exchange for sacred songs. They called him Grandfather and Friend. The Insect deputies tried to get their songs back. First Man's armor was invulnerable, and they only succeeded in injuring each other.

First Man rolled up his armor. Coyote and Spider Ant went about and reported back to First Man that there was much suffering and misery, and Pot Carrier Beetle said that he did not want his handiwork destroyed. First Man then blew smoke in all the directions and swallowed it each time, thus removing the "power of evil from the people of the First World, the Insect People."

This power now entered into First Man and the others of the original nine Holy People. Coyote reported that all seemed well.

First Man, using Zig-Zag Lightning, Straight Lightning, Rainbow, and Sun Ray, tried to bring about an upward movement, but he could not. Finally he made a wand and set it upright. From the bottom upward it was made of Jet, Turquoise, Abalone, White Shell, and Red-White Stone. On each side of it were four footprints. The people stood on these and were carried up to the Third World. "As a matter of course, First Man never neglected to carry all his powers from one world to another."

From the uneasy but not violent beginnings in the primal darkness until now, little conflict has been evidenced. There have been moments of exploration and moments of quiescence, moments of forgetfulness and moments of remembering. The maternal encompassing egg has broken, and individual beings now possess the substance: Pot Carrier's pots, First Man's rolled-up cloud columns. Evil has been recognized as a "given," as part of the ancestor-creator and the Holy Ones. Coyote the changeling, the disturber, has emerged as a vital psychic force. The dark world has yielded to the world of danger. Yet all this has come about in relative calmness and rhythmic slowness of pace, until the earth-shaking of this chamber of the Second World begins.

Clashes and shatterings cannot be successful until the roots are deepened. Every creation is a statement about the growth of our awareness of reality, a sense of what fills our emptiness. A creation starting deep in the earth is a creation concerned first of all with the solid and rooted continuity of being. The original stress is not on the fluctuating and unpredictable, but on the unseen foundations. Out of this comes the desire to know, the longing to become. The infant and the animal begin in this world. And each of us must return to understand and incorporate this world if our consciousness is to have the ground it needs. Problems with the mother umbilicus are unavoidable, even under optimum conditions. Every man and woman, as part of maturation, seeks to become independent, just as a plant stretches away from the earth where its seed began to sprout and seeks to blossom and bear fruit in the free air. Yet without the nourishing soil the plant dies. Without a connection to the maternal root principle the personality withers. Our racial origins, our biological inheritance, even our difficult familial connections, are parts of us. I have known many Americans who could not find themselves until they journeyed in physical fact to the place of their ancestors. When, in one way or another, this gap between us and our sources is bridged, this hole in our inner earth filled, then the process of individuation can proceed.

The pace now changes in the myth. This part of the Second World is the home of all the Feline People: wolves, wildcats, foxes, badgers, mountain lions. Different groups live at the various direction points. "All the houses were of different shapes and these people were at war with each other; they were tricksters and makers of arrows, and the travellers joined the various factions," as Haile renders it. The peaceful evolving now is replaced by conflict, upheaval, aggression, antagonism, and destruction. The power of the possession of the mother pots and of the light columns has become too great, perhaps. Moreover, once the earth-shaking quality of the vital power of the Red-White Stone has been recognized, there must of necessity be a consequent time of eruption. When the preconscious self pushes for expression too soon, destructiveness and inflation are almost inevitable. That is to say, from the point of view of unthinking nature every evolutionary stage of self-determination and self-consciousness is in this sense "too soon," and that which stands on the side of natural inertia arms itself against that which stands on the side of emergence.

The Feline People as named are virtually all predatory animals, usually solitary and sly, and often night prowlers. Our common speech shows vividly certain estimates of catness. "Jealous as a cat." "Lonely as a cat." "Smug as a cat." "She is catty" (sarcastic, gossipy, cruel). The domestic cat, for all its wondrously sinuous grace and loving containment, is also a clever bargainer for our attention and really cares not at all for our hurt feelings. An Egyptian text relates that the sun's eye rebelled against the sun, withdrew from Egypt to Nubia, and lived as a lioness or lynx who only with great difficulty was prevailed upon to return.[17] This lioness was sometimes referred to as the "angry goddess." A mother-goddess of the sea, in Babylonian creation myth, created monsters from herself in order to revenge her husband's death. One of these was the Great-lion (angry spirit), a panther-footed serpent dragon, and one was called the Gruesome Hound.[18] Jung has stated: "Lions, like all wild animals, indicate latent affects. The lion plays an important part in alchemy and has much the same meaning. It is a 'fiery' animal, an emblem of the devil, and stands for the danger of being swallowed by the unconscious."[19]

What does this point toward inside man? After any extended or sustained progress, apparently there comes a state of being where formerly positive values appear as negative, trying to pull us backward to an earlier condition. The Feline People seem to be, at this point, the regressive pull of the unrestrained animal drives, "natural inertia" against "spiritual" discipline. These drives were harmless enough in the dark beginning world where everything was dim and unconscious. Only a hum of restless movement then filled the twilight. The restlessness grew and pushed to change, solidified and focused through Ant People, Pot Carrier Beetle, Locust, Coyote, Sphinx Moth. And now there begins a striving for control between the unconscious warring instincts and the current protagonist for consciousness, First Man. The enemy has good as well as bad effects, however. Newcomb asserts that the various cats—mountain lion, lynx, leopard, wildcat—are sometimes shown as bearers of the gift of medicinal herbs, sometimes as messengers or informers.[20] In this myth, certainly, despite their negative and aggressive behavior, the Feline People do give to First Man valuable gifts of sacred songs.

In the development of a culture, certain attitudes of greed, aggression, unrestrained individualism, must be brought to heel if the culture is to survive. So also in an individual life. Infancy ends as the child begins to have an ego which can enter into choices and decisions. And as adults, we need to be aware that each new step in growth and discovery has in it always the danger of the autonomy of the down-drag of nature. What happens in the myth may happen to us. The irritations and restlessnesses join forces with the half-savage and autonomous emotional demands and erupt into open conflict. Each part is against each other part. All parts are against ego consciousness. Intense emotions are for this reason splendid barometers of internal conflicts and autonomies.

An instance of this is a married couple whose relationship was primarily that of brother and sister rather than husband and wife. Realizing their impoverishment, both came to analysis, wanting love to come forth in its full maturity. The normal instincts were aroused from the unconscious; the brother-sister masks fell away. All should have gone smoothly if growth into love were a direct progression. But it is not. As the emotions and affects were set free, war was declared between the woman's jealous possessiveness and the man's polygamous pulls. She resented any other woman, and he was angry over any demand. The ancient animal needs, so long repressed, threatened to take over the relationship where half-conscious friendship had previously been the leader. Only the best efforts of both partners and both analysts eventually helped the marriage to a place of more conscious and rewarding confrontation.

In regard to intensity of reaction, while too much intellect may sometimes be healed by a temporary swing to the realm of unbridled emotionalism, a condition of psychic ignorance cannot be so treated. Instinct, although it may sometimes defeat overconsciousness, is quite helpless to defeat semiconsciousness. This type of futile struggle, between half-conscious forward thrusts and aroused instincts, is often manifested by the ways in which our uncreative behavior resists attack. It is as if the neurotic condition did not want to be overcome, as if it aggressively "smelled out" any efforts to destroy it. It seems to appropriate to itself and for its own autonomous and negative purposes all urges toward growth. The result is a temporary stalemate in which defensive conflict replaces constructive change.

Change does come, however, and often for the better.

This mythological situation occurs in the *Popol Vuh* when, after the preforms of man have been worked at by the gods, a trickster-giant (Vucub-Caquix) and his two sons turn inflated and destructive; they are greedy, arrogant, and as bloodthirsty as the cats.[21] But the theme of transformation of malevolent to benevolent is found here as well as in the Navaho myth; some part (or all) of each giant is turned into something else: maize, mountain, earth. Indians of the Andes told of animal-like giants who finally angered the gods and were replaced by a new race of beings.[22] Ancient Mexican creation stories told of earthquakes which destroyed the giants.[23] In a like manner the Norse giants were turned into earth. The battle of the Titans against the Olympian gods is a parallel in Greek myth.[24] The "old" gods, sprung from archaic parents, children of a devouring Kronos, tried to push down the "new" gods of consciousness. The Olympians knew they could not win unaided against the forces of unconsciousness. Led by Zeus, they were helped not only by the arrows of Heracles (and Dionysus, say some tales) but also by the hundred-armed giants released from imprisonment in Tartarus. So consciousness must come to terms with unconscious contents, must move to meet the attack from the powers of darkness.

We must see consciousness, first of all, as our collected knowledge built up through example and teaching from childhood onward. We come to "know" about specifics and generalities as we are exposed to the "knowing" of family, nation, race. This conscious mind is vital to us as we fight our way forward. Yet it can become top-heavy, even as the inert weight of unconsciousness can become an almost irresistible drag. Consciousness—the Olympian gods, First Man—must come to struggle with unconsciousness, and in so doing *both* conscious and unconscious realms are altered. The conscious ego is given shape by the new things rising up, while the nonego forces are tempered by the effect of consciousness. The psychological sin of growth-resistant unconsciousness seems always to threaten our emergent life. The Felines, like the giants, war and kill, cheat and defy. And like the giants, the Felines have to be outwitted, reduced to more human and more functional size. That which is too big, too inhuman, too unrestrained, must give way if the human "I" is to take its rightful place.

Because no Luciferian figure is all negative, the first step of the bearers of ego consciousness is to find some point of contact and thus to relate victor to victim, the "biter" to the "bitten." In the *Popol Vuh*, for example, this point of contact is seen in the fact that one of the male twin divinities is himself catlike, has possibly certain darker "moon" qualities. In the Navaho myth, First Man possesses some Felines as guardians of his home. In both cases, a positive and vital animal strength is available to help carry the tremendous burden of self-searching. It is a kind of psychological homeopathy which enables the still-forming ego to withstand the dangerous poison of its absolute opposite.

At this point in the myth the clash between alien forces grows in intensity. Fiercely the enemy Felines try to injure or destroy First Man. But his power is greater. And his method of winning is psychologically quite sound. He kills only a few of each group of Feline People who attack him, thus weakening their destructive power, but preserving the chances of their positive contributions.

For they have sacred songs and prayers which First Man needs and which he receives in exchange for his reviving of those killed. Once again the divine nature of the attacker is apparent. Here is no final repressive annihilation of the dark and dangerous aspects of life, but a regulation of them by harnessing their values to the purposes of creation. This transfer of strength is similar to those previously mentioned mythic episodes where giants are shattered and their fragments become stones and mountains. The breaking of bread in the mass, the eating of the god (Dionysos) in a loaf, the shattering of giants, the warlike wresting of sacred songs from the Feline People—all these are ways of changing too great a vitality into assimilable food for spiritual growth.

Dreams, as mythic statements, can offer contemporary examples. Sometimes the shadowy, dark, and unfamiliar negativities of ourselves threaten to take over and must be "brought to heel." A man who was much afraid of his own unexpressed but smoldering hostility dreamed:

> I go into a splendid palace, like Versailles. A big stupid man, very powerful, attacks me suddenly and starts to strangle me. Instead of fighting back, I call him brother. The big fellow lets go, begins to cry. Then we shake hands, and he comes with me.

The man needed to assimilate his unredeemed masculine strength, needed to have its sacred power for his own ego development rather than to continue being strangled by unregenerate rage. Affirmation of genuine purpose was the solution given him by the dream. For a woman, the image of her inner masculine principle frequently is the destructive "giant" who must be tamed. The following dream of a young woman who tyrannized her friends and misused her genuinely creative talents is an illustration:

> In a large house with many people, I seemed to be trying to do lots of important work but a huge giant of a man kept getting in my way and pushing me around. He looked sort of crazy and I began to be afraid. From somewhere a voice said, "Give him something to do."

Here the dream solution was to find ways in everyday life to utilize the wasted and thus dangerous energy of the active principle of direction. In both the man and the woman a real vitality was being ignored, and because it was ignored it was beginning to erupt. Both "giants" demanded a more conscious relationship with the ego, in exchange for which they would serve the Self.

In the Navaho myth the Insects, those restless unconscious longings, again move to center stage. They have broken free from their attachment to the Feline People, the autonomous instincts, but they nonetheless continue to resist any conscious direction. They try belligerently to get back the sacred songs.

If we are driven by our own irritable urges to seek beyond where we are, it is likely that we may fall eventually under the spell of heretofore unknown and unbridled drives which draw us into deep inner conflict. Our own sense of direction, ·if strong enough, will recognize there is value here. It will also sense that it cannot stay in this chaotic and irresponsible form. Yet our directionless urgency has found a welcome release in the emotional battle, and we are loath to let it be disciplined or channeled. A good example is the alcoholic who resists mightily the relinquishing of his artificial power in exchange for a more sober security. And in his stubborn attempt to hold onto this power he only succeeds in hurting other parts of himself.

So it is with the Insect beings at this point in the Navaho myth. Their arrows cannot penetrate First Man's armor, and they only wound each other. In a discussion of witchcraft, Kluckhohn and Leighton write: "The Navaho theory under all circumstances is that if the intended victim is too strong or too well protected the witch's evil backfires upon himself." [25] Inevitably this must lead either to destruction or to some working together of parts.

A new sequence of movement now occurs in the myth, combining the thrusting vertical and the exploratory horizontal. First Man does not turn from the scene of havoc and his victory, departing in arrogant retaliation. In removing his armor, he opens himself to whatever has happened as a result of the conflict between instinct and consciousness. He has subdued the autonomy in its negative attacks, but has not annihilated its energies. And the conquered instincts are deeply suffering, piteously humbled.

When we in our battle for consciousness accomplish a like victory over ourselves in our partial nature, our instinctive processes are truly, as the myth says, in anguish.

The cruelty and insensitivity of "I want" (and "I demand" and "my urges must always be expressed now") have to be reduced to a state of inability to function. Their previous unconscious inflation and antisocial action have to be sternly, even harshly, dealt with. If at this point we walk away, leaving our animal nature to perish, we jump from one partialness to another equally harmful. We do not achieve a conscious advance.

So also with a culture. There is always the great danger that resistances and reformations, despite the genuine needs inciting them, become rigidities. That which was to be reformed is left to die on the field of battle. It has been so with Western man. His commendable and necessary desire for increased awareness of and control over his world has resulted in the suffering and death of his warm human feelings. Coming at a period of history when pagan, Judaic, Greek, Oriental influences were all converging and creating something of a rip tide in the human sea, Jesus of Nazareth brought a sharp challenge to the individual to reach toward a new and revolutionary level of self-awareness. This challenge, however, grew old and staid and became the comfortable Christian theology of the Middle Ages. Renaissance man arose against his too ordered universe and replaced it in a tremendous resurgence of individual knowledge and particularized achievement, replete at first with feeling and love. But in the conflict between Medieval love of God and Renaissance love of man, Eros itself was somehow lost. The scope of a Da Vinci who could encompass religion, art, myth, science, was narrowed to the "brass instrument" mentality of the nineteenth century. The penultimate stage is the atom-splitting, technological, space-racing present century. Perhaps, however, as an American poet wrote wistfully, "There is nowhere to go from the top of a mountain but down, my dear." [26] Perhaps now we must, as nations and as individuals, go down once more to the stable of our nativity where the only absolute is reborn life.

The one in the myth who must now immerse himself

in the fullness of what has taken place is Coyote, assisted by Spider Ant. First Man asked what was wrong. Coyote said, "Oh, well, they probably repeated what they tried before, but instead of injuring us their arrows turned upon themselves. . . ." "We have visited the people round about," said Spider Ant, "and have seen misery everywhere. Have pity on them and allow us to depart. . . ." "Well," said First Man, "let me see what I can do while you step outside." Meanwhile, Coyote went off to the four directions, turning the color of each direction as he went, and returned to report the enormity of the suffering. As a wanderer and a disturber, Coyote absorbed the sacred colors in the First World. This movement brought the human and the divine into initial relationship. Now again it is the wise and persistent scoundrel, man's potential creatureliness, who moves from point to point and sees the suffering of the defeated.

It is our creaturely imperfection, the affirmation of our incompleteness and our weakness, which enables us to be kind. If we are to grow, surely we must do battle and just as surely we must receive the wounds of battle. Love and tenderness must follow both for the victorious and the vanquished parts of the psyche. Otherwise the battle has no meaning. To love ourselves is to care about the fate of each and every aspect of ourselves, even those which have been recalcitrant and destructive. If we resent and hate our willfulness with which we have fought, we find ourselves unable to proceed further, although we may have "won" the fight. For we have not yet accepted our own frailties. We have not let ourselves look with compassion on our suffering.

A sense of compassion and mercy seems to be an essential part of many aftermaths of cosmic destruction. After the Babylonian deluge, it is written, Ea, god of the deep, said, "Now punish the sinner for his sins and the evil doer for his evil deed, but be merciful and do not destroy all mankind." [27] And Kuan Yin, the Chinese Buddhist goddess of mercy, is said to have received her name because, hearing cries of anguish from mankind, she was moved by pity and compassion and turned back before she entered heaven.[28] Likewise Coyote takes on the sacred colors as he moves about amid the pain and misery. The light goes with him into the darkness. This is true compassion.

Because Coyote goes into the world, and because he brings back to First Man a recognition of the true state of things, the way is clear for the final movements of transformation at this level. Beetle and Spider Ant, representatives of the early insect restlessness which became negative and clung to the autonomous instincts, dare to come and plead for release. "We want to leave this place where we see misery everywhere, have pity, and let us go." This is the sad and wonderful cry of those who were lost and have been found again—sad because pain and conflict seem inevitable for growth, and wonderful because the misery has been allowed to recognize itself and so to be set free. In a small and primitive way, this scene has some of the poignancy and greatness of the return of the prodigal son: "For your brother was dead, and is alive again; and was lost, and is found." [29]

Nowhere is the strange role of evil clearer than at this next moment in the mythic drama. Evil portents at a preceding time led into darkness and danger. The Insect beings risked themselves by moving into unknown ground, by letting themselves be drawn into the strife with the Felines, by playing with sorcery and black magic. If they had not, if they had ventured nothing and avoided the dangerous, they would have stopped their own learning progression. Evil, in this way, is seen to be both the unavoidable blundering and weakness of an undirected irritation and the very necessary backward action which alone leads to a new wholeness. When the evil has served its purpose for the time being, it is taken *back*. Note well that it is not taken *away*. First Man makes smoke, blows it to each of the four directions, then swallows the smoke again, removing the evil from the people. He puts it into himself, into his feminine counterpart, First Woman, and into the nine Holy People. Thus the evil, as a part of life, is carried in sacredness and safety by those who can bear the weight. If we could but learn this—not to fear or to flee the darkness and negativity, but to permit them to be borne eventually by the divine in us—then, perhaps, we would also know of evil, "when to use it and when to withhold it," as First Man says later on.

When the time is at hand for the movement upward to the next world, First Man finds that nothing happens until the right configuration is found. It is important to see how often the Navaho myths emphasize this fact of the healing power of a total situation or configuration, as different from a partial knowledge. This is to say, no matter how great the vision and no matter how profoundly rich the carrier of that vision, it cannot be actualized until all things are ready for its actualization.

Now is the time, we may say, for the changes in us to show. Now we should be able to step forth boldly and without hesitation into a new life. It is not so simple. It does not come effortlessly and suddenly, this transition, for us or for First Man. The great cosmic powers of Lightning, Rainbow, Sun Ray remain virtually motionless. Only that made by hands, carefully wrought of the four sacred stones beginning with the black and crowned by the red-white, can lift the people upward. It is as if, in this mythological prevision of psychic fullness, we were being told that each step must be thoughtfully taken; that the godlike experience comes only when we are willing to begin in the dark unknown and proceed to the final purifying; that the apex of each unique cycle is the fruitful paradox of dawn and danger. So the next stage is entered. So also the gods are there with all their powers—and nothing is left behind.

IV

Witchcraft and Holiness

Summary

USE AND MISUSE OF EVIL

When the people emerged into the Third World (eighth chamber)—the Yellow World—they found "one single old man and his wife and another old fellow" living there. These were Salt Man and Salt Woman and Fire God. Also there were all kinds of Snake People, including various colored snakes who were evil.

All the wicked Snake People and the others "looked at, and studied one another while First Scolder (Coyote), unconcerned, roamed about to give the place the lookover. 'What sort of a fellow is that, boys,' they said, 'that goes about here with no respect for anything!'"

First Man then put yellow and red-and-yellow streaks in the east to keep the white column of light from rising. The people, alarmed, asked four times what was wrong. Finally Dontso the Messenger Fly was prevailed upon to tell them. He said that the streaks represented Emergence, pollen and vegetation, and diseases. Owl, Fox, Wolf, and Wildcat addressed the people. Apparently some gift was necessary for First Man before he would remove the obstacles. "They could think of nothing valuable at first." Then Horned Rattlesnake (Big Snake), who "carried a perfect (nonperforated) shell disk and horns on his head," gave to First Man this perfect shell as an offering. The

streaks were removed, and the light column arose in the east.
The people accused First Man of being malicious. He replied, "It is true, my grandchildren. I am filled with evil; yet there is a time to employ it and another to withhold it."

IN the three major versions of the Navaho creation myth—recorded by Father Berard Haile, Mary Wheelwright, and Washington Matthews—there are interesting differences in the accounts of the sequence of the worlds. Both sequence and number of worlds vary. As Reichard states, "The number of worlds is hypothetical, there being little agreement about it; myth furnishes details of four underworlds, of the sky immediately above, and of one still higher, Land-beyond-the-sky." [1] There is, however, a tendency to consider our world, the present world, as the fifth one, although this is not always explicitly stated. Also the colors attached to these worlds vary with different informants. For example:

World	Haile-Wheelwright	Matthews	Klah-Wheelwright	Oakes (Feather Chant)
First	"Dark underworld"	Red	"Running-pitch place"	Black
Second	Red	Blue	Blue	Blue
Third	Yellow	Yellow	Yellow	Yellow
Fourth	Blue	Black and white	(White?)	White
Fifth	White	?	?	?

The one clear-cut agreement is that the Third World is yellow. This seems to make it of special importance in numerical sequence, as if yellow and whatever meaning it carries could not come elsewhere. The color yellow, judged from evidence in the various Navaho myths, is related to seeds and to fruit. It is the color of the west, which is where the immortals are said to live. According to Newcomb yellow is "a color of spiritual blessing and also immediate physical well-being, and seems to carry fewer ills, along with the good, than any of the other four." [2] In rites and sandpaintings, yellow cornmeal symbolizes fertility, and yellow pollen indicates blessing. Reichard feels it is more particularly related to "the power of wild vegetation" due to its association with cattail rush pollen.[3] Yellow is also the color of female corn. Thus it seems as if the fructifying power of the primitive earth had to come, in the upward reaching, between the groping struggles of the lower worlds and the more expanding life of the higher worlds.

The Haile Emergence myth has a comparatively short Third World history, yet a highly significant and strange one in which the color yellow has a dominant position. When First Man, the other Holy People, and the beings from the lower levels arrived in the Third World they found Salt Man and Salt Woman there. (The myth also mentions Fire God again, who appears to be rather omnipresent in moments of crisis and transition.) Whereas the Second World (of red) was populated by Felines, this world is populated by eight kinds of Snakes, including the Great Horned Rattlesnake. Coyote establishes relationship by wandering about in his clumsy way and getting to know everyone.

Once more the stage is set for a new drama. The little Insect beings, their restless antennae quivering and sensitive, together with the eight Holy Ones, images of man's later sacredness, enter into a phase where fructification and generation are the dominant cosmic principles. The First World beings have already come a long, arduous way. The blind and confining darkness of irritable unknowing has been transcended. The mother realm in its absolute undifferentiation has been left behind. The masculine possibility of light is now possessed by First Man, and the demanding instincts are partially understood. Yet the mother aspect is present in a new form as old Salt

Woman, said to have been made of some skin rubbed from First Man's armpits. Great is the Navaho wisdom which does not make judgments that upper levels are "better" than lower ones, does not permit the leaving behind of essential ingredients. Although the feminine principle must be transcended in its overpowering primal possessiveness, this does not mean that it can be renounced. It must be there as earth, as salt of the earth, as in the composition of the life's blood.

In our journey from level to level of our own nature, we often have to confront the disturbing fact that what we thought lay behind us still walks beside us patiently. And in our dismay we fail to recognize the growth it has undergone, the new clothes it wears. The first restless rise of dim longing leads us up and away from the comfortable mothering darkness. We must take on the burden of humanness and relate to the light as part of our ancestral heritage. We must risk ourselves in challenging the autonomy of our instinctual drives. Having done this, having come this far, we must not be surprised to meet once more the mother, for the archetypal Mother, as Neumann demonstrates definitively, has manifold phases and paradoxical meanings.[4] (This principle is discussed more fully in the later section on Changing Woman, pp. 174ff.)

A woman whose mother had recently died had this dream: "Mother appeared before me in dark robes. First she was very tall, then she receded and grew smaller and dimmer. Someone told me, or I knew, that she had gone to the Mothers." Some months later came the following dream: "In a place like a Greek temple. A woman, maybe a priestess, dressed in Grecian robes, came with a cedar branch and led me into some sort of initiation room." One form of the mother falls back into the darkness to be replaced by another. The nourishing but possessive personal mother to whom one is related as a child must be let go. The mother principle in its transforming, initiating quality, to which we are related as novices but not as children, then appears. Such is the endless cycle of the archetypal images, turning like the wheel of fate.

Moreover, having struggled with the evil of autonomous urges, we must not be surprised if evil is still present. Not infrequently a person bursts out, "But I thought I had dealt with that problem! I guess I haven't gotten anywhere at all!" This is not so. It is only that the archetypal figures, in their endless round, cross the individual spiral path again and again in everchanging guises, but each time at a higher place.

Witness this new stage. Evil is present in Third World even more emphatically than before. And how can this be? Did not First Man, the carrier of the power of light, take upon himself the task of subduing the split-off hostility of the Felines? Precisely this act, however, led to the fresh evils. Because First Man's throwing out and swallowing of the smoke was a sacrificial rite, the penalty must now be paid for sacrifice. First Man has become both "priest" and "victim." He bears the shadow within himself. Apparently, according to the myth, he can begin to redeem himself only if he fully uses his dark magic to increase his sacred power and thus also to increase the power of the others under his leadership.

The Great Horned Rattlesnake, from whom First Man is to get the perfect shell, is surely the symbolic representation of earth energy in heroic size. The snake is generally in Navaho myths a feared personage, unpredictable and dangerous; it also serves as a helper, a guardian spirit, a lifter of heroes. Great Rattlesnake is similar to other horned beings in mythology. American Indian lore is replete with examples of the snake as spirit-being. In fact, Radin asserts that the most characteristic spirit creature in the Americas is "the widespread Water-Spirit, also known as the Horned Snake and the Plumed Serpent. He unquestionably belongs to the old strata of belief, and, although adopted by shaman everywhere, has undergone almost no recasting." [5]

While Radin considers this Horned Snake as more or less malign, others like Barbeau feel the Plumed or Horned Serpents are "helpful sky monsters controlling the waters and thunders." [6] The Horned Snake is found in myths of the Apache Indians, the Pueblo groups, and in Mexico as Quetzlcoatl. A Coos Indian myth[7] tells of a young girl who finds a tiny snake, makes a pet of it, only to have it grow to a huge size, develop two great horns, and supply her with enough to make her rich. And until fairly recent times the Zuñi Indians had an elaborate ritual of initiation involving the use of a five-foot-long black and white serpent with feather plumes arising from its head.[8]

In Navaho myths there are many examples of serpents playing varying roles;[9] sometimes they are guardians of the homes of the gods, sometimes holy ones living in their own abodes, sometimes connecting links with the water under the earth. Navaho snake deities are, for the most part, seen as dangerous, but with great potentials for transformation and healing. These potentials are now needed by First Man. He may have coped with the nature energy in its dissociated form (Feline People), but he must possess the talisman of that nature energy in its more earthbound and sacred form. His method is to stop the white column of light from rising in the east by placing a yellow and a red-and-yellow streak across the white column. Haile says that at one point the witchcraft group (the nine) blew red stone and yellow stone at the east, as part of the preparation.

It appears that a decision was sought to let the appearance of yellow on the eastern horizon indicate health, growth, and all that is good. The appearance of the red stone color on the horizon would indicate . . . smallpox, . . . big or whooping cough, . . . hunger and all evil. The nine-group interfered saying that they would have their own mind about this. But yellow is always good, red stone . . . always bad, which seems to imply that disease is due to the witchery of the nine-group, and a red-streaked horizon will portend this. A yellow horizon will portend health and prosperity.[10]

Dawn, purification, renewal, rebirth, cannot proceed. The quality of sustenance—earth, fruits, creatureliness—and the quality of the danger of the earthy nature must first be thought upon, attended to, and intermingled. After a period of ignorance and darkness, of troubled waiting, Dontso the divine emissary says that First Man must have a gift, and the magic talisman is given by the Horned Serpent. How dark the unconscious problem is at this point is revealed by the fact that all creatures of the night—Owl, Fox, Wolf, Wildcat—are the mediators. The moon and its light are present in the perfect White Shell disk which is offered.

How often we are confronted by a like situation. We have struggled to overcome hostilities and resistances, we have reached a plateau (so we believe) where at last some fruit of our labor may be visible. Then the light ceases. We are confused and angry. Only patiently asking and listening, turning to the voices of the unconscious psyche, can help us to know what is needed. At such a time we want to rise without hindrance into a reborn state; we are restive under the demands of time and space and the insistence that we attend to and accept our earthly and limited humanity. We want to be free and "good" and redeemed from natural law. And we cannot be. We have to learn the awesome truth hidden in those intensely dramatic words of First Man, "It is true, my grandchildren. I am filled with evil; yet there is a time to employ it and another to withhold it." Because First Man rightly employed his "evil"—even as he had rightly taken it back into himself before—he gained the serpent power. That is to say, he gained in earth fertility and strength from the *masculine* snake divinity.

The nature of this divinity is revealed not only by the previous references to American Indian symbolism but also by a consideration of some ancient traditions. Horned bull gods are well known, and many heroes have been portrayed with horns (such as Michelangelo's Moses, and legends of Dionysos as a horned child). Bayley has indicated that there is a very ancient idea that horns exercised some "potent, evil-averting, and protective influence." [11] In Egypt, the sacred horned serpent was sometimes called "the horned shining light," and, says Bayley, "the Egyptians affirmed that Ptah, the Lord of Truth, emerged from an egg that came out from the mouth of Amun-Knepth, the True and Perfect Serpent." [12] Avalon, in *The Serpent Power*, draws similarities between Kundalini yoga concepts and American Indian ideas. Hurakan (of Maya myth) is, he says, Kundalini.[13] Kundalini Shakti "is spoken of as coiled because She is likened to a serpent . . . which, when resting and sleeping, lies coiled; and because the nature of Her power is spiraline, manifesting itself as such in the worlds—the spheroids or 'eggs of Brahma.'" [14] In Kundalini yoga, spinal column and serpent are related, and to have "serpent power" is to have the lowest body areas connected to the highest by way of "wakening" the coiled snake in the depths and permitting its fertility to work upward and permeate the entire body.

This same sort of interweaving and counterpoint between First Man and Horned Rattlesnake, of black magic and white magic, of loss and gain, calls to mind some of the events in the Old Testament history of the children of Israel. When Moses desired to lead his people out of bondage, the Lord gave him powerful magic whereby he brought plagues and evil days upon the people of Egypt. For a time the Egyptian magicians "did the same with their secret arts," matching magic for magic. But Moses' power from the Lord proved stronger, and Pharaoh pleaded to have the plagues lifted. However, when the plagues were taken back, "the Lord made Pharaoh obstinate, so that he would not let the Israelites go." Only after the death of the first-born was the exodus from Egypt possible. Much later, the Israelites were punished by the Lord with a plague of poisonous serpents. And then the Lord helped Moses make a bronze serpent which healed those who looked upon it.[15]

This highly charged exchange of trials and terrors, with sorcery and miracle as weapons in the struggle for freedom, clearly shows the use of evil to prevail over evil.[16] The Lord God, Yahweh, seems to alternate between helping Moses and hindering him, between loving the Israelites and then sending serpents to destroy them. But the magic of Yahweh—in the staff of Moses—proves stronger than the magic of the Egyptians. And the great bronze serpent is the antidote to the snake plague.

What is the meaning of this apparent ambivalence of the gods? Surely Yahweh could have said, as First Man does, "I am filled with evil; yet there is a time to employ it and another to withhold it." What does this say of the nature of the divine? First of all, it indicates that the divine is not dualistic, but holds within itself all possibilities of darkness and of light. First Man stopped the east light deliberately; but had he not done so he would not have obtained the treasure of the great Horned Rattlesnake. Completion, greater fullness, a wider grasp of the multitudinous aspects of life—these are what man and the gods must strive for. Not perfection and "goodness"; never these. It is a very striking feature of this primitive Indian myth—primitive in the sense of not coming from a people of a high degree of cultural consciousness—that this profound concept of the gods is present.

The Navaho myth does not, to be sure, pose the moral problems of the Old Testament story of Moses and Yahweh, because the latter involves the complicated relationship between man and God at a more advanced level of growth, raising the question of mutual responsibility for consciousness. One cannot yet, in the Indian myth, trace the subtle nuances of the border lines of the divine awareness; one cannot seek the solution here to the cosmic unconsciousness as it sometimes seems to stand on the side of evil. For First Man is only a primal prevision of the male principle, actualizing the image of the outreaching spirit of man. He is the "first ancestor," the first heritage of man, and not the more differentiated paradox of the Old Testament Yahweh. Nonetheless, even in this episode, it is apparent that darkness and light must be eternally juxtaposed and interwoven if the movement which is creation can go forward.

It is also made clear that the employing and the withholding of evil are a part of the "mysterium" of the psychical collective forces and of our relationship to that mystery. It must not be forgotten that this particular version of the Emergence belongs to the Evil Way, or Hotchonji, and thus is concerned with fighting against evil. To employ or to withhold evil is to be aware of the facts that both light and darkness are necessary, that both are encountered as part of the eternally changing flow of an individual life, and that we must deal with both at appropriate seasons and in appropriate ways.

We of the present era have a particularly acute problem because we have tended to see the material world as primary. We have become accustomed to taking a one-sidedly rational point of view, assuming that "light" and "goodness" would prevail if only we could know about all things technologically. The "dark," negative, evil component is from this point of view the result of nothing but lack of factual knowledge. And as long as we cling to this comfortable and comforting faith, we cannot say, with the 139th Psalm, "the light and the darkness are alike unto Thee." Nor will we participate in the mystery.

It is difficult to judge what is positive and what is negative in us, and it takes great courage to face and to endure our negative side. A general confession of the unknown and concealed aspects of ourselves, saying we are "filled with evil," is relatively easy compared to the heroic act of saying, "Here, and here, and here the shadows live in me."

The mystery of the serpent is more creatively ours when we can begin to recognize what the consequences of our shadows are or may be in our immediate existence. What things have we done to ourselves and to others, and how do we feel about our actions? Where we recoil with pain, where we are burdened by guilt—there our darkest shadows lie waiting. To learn to "employ" and to "withhold," so to be able to get from the Horned Rattlesnake his treasure, is to dare to confront our specific shadows, guilt, and responsibility.

And how is it when we do not do this? A young man whose marriage was failing primarily because of his lovable but maddening irresponsibility had this dream:

> I am going on a journey into a new country. I ride my horse through a forest and am getting near an undiscovered city when a savage native, dark-skinned and jeering, rides towards me and blocks my way. I feel I should fight him, but I jump from my horse and run away.

He could not face the vicious shadow of the "lovable boy," could not assume responsibility for his own evil. He not only ran away psychologically but in actual fact deserted his wife and children and fled. The mystery was rejected.

Primitive man (as also our own less sophisticated and irrational side) realizes the collective unconscious dark mystery as primal. "Before the world was, I am." So the primitive, with the undifferentiated wisdom of Everyman's inwardness, not only works to ward off these psychological forces in their negative aspects but reaches out to help them begin to play and move in their helpful aspects. Therefore, in this myth, the alternating activity and quiescence of the "evil" processes can be construed as an intrinsic part of the opening up of a cooperative two-way road between not-conscious psychical powers and our awareness of them.

Twentieth-century Western man needs to see this value of the use of "evil" in order to wrest the treasure of discrimination from the archaic undivided oneness. Otherwise he will be engulfed in unconsciousness or in psychosis. An American woman in her early thirties had the following dream:

> I am in a great underground chamber seeking for an unknown treasure. Suddenly I see a huge serpent coming toward me from one direction, and a sabre-tooth tiger from the opposite direction. I am terrified, and fear I will be devoured by them. Somehow I realize that, if I can get them to fight, I will be able to escape. I wait until they are both very near, then I run away and they attack each other.

This flight is not like that of the young man previously discussed. It is not necessary to know more about this woman to see that the primal forces had to be subdued and also that the dreamer herself could not do it. Feline and serpent had to confront each other and thus reduce their own fearsomeness. In the myth, First Man himself coped with the evils of each. In the dreamer's awareness of the dangers, and in her quite deliberate timing of flight, she partakes somewhat indirectly of the wisdom of First Man.

First Man functions in and through us insofar as we are willing to abide by, and act upon, the wisdom imparted to us in dreams, outer situations, mythological events. If we try to sense and to interpret the myth as a description of events within ourselves, we need to assume that the individual ego, the "I," is the one who reacts and learns from the myth. In the same way, in dreams, the ego is the dreamer. Thus in the dream just cited, the dreamer's realization of the danger and of how to ward it off comes from her personal ego strength; while in the previously given dream of the young man, the ego was weak and could not cope with the situation.

First Man is the inner wisdom, paradoxical in nature, which must be listened to by the slowly growing ego. We must have the humility and security to follow the "little glimmerings and shinings" of light in the soul, as Pennington wrote.[17] We must be listeners and followers. We cannot—in fact we must not—assume the role of First Man. Our task is one of conscious reconciliation and mediation, of patiently bringing into everyday circumstance our growing knowledge of what happens in the deeper and darker levels of our being. And by separating out from the vague oneness of the mother-beginnings, by renouncing the desire for perfection, by accepting the presence of evil in ourselves as a quality to be dealt with as part of creatureliness, we can perhaps begin to live as human beings in a human world.

Summary

THE CREATION HOGAN

First Man placed the sacred stones in the four directions with the Red-White Stone in the northeast, breathed upon them, and a white hogan arose on five poles. Into this four-storied hogan all the people came. Coyote kept moving about in the northeast sector, asking what was going on and muttering to himself. First Man assigned places to everyone. He made the four Medicine Pouches for the Upward-Reaching (Emergence) ceremony. Songs were sung. First Man distributed to the nine Holy Ones "all his medicine, good and bad."

The people wanted to move upward, so First Man tried to bring light, but Coyote had interfered with it, for he was angry at being called Wanderer or Scolder. Four sacred stones were offered Coyote by various persons, and they called to him as He-who-calls-the-daylight, and other titles. And "Coyote untied the pillars of light at the east, south, west and north, and so the Sahd (world or holy council) functioned again and became holy. First Man then took down the Hogan, rolled it into a small ball, and laid it aside."

First Man put the five Holy Stones in the center, and they carried the people, who were still evil, into the next world.

IN the beginning, even when the first dark world was as yet a restless and pathless place and the first beings had not begun their upward journey, there still was the skeletal structure of fourfold containment. The four mounds at the four compass points seemed a promise of what could be. At each subsequent level of unfolding in the myth the sacred quadrant appeared, increasing in fullness and vertical reach. Again it comes, this time immediately after First Man's astounding statement about his own nature. Now it is not only a space stretching outward and upward but a place defined and vibrant with life.

If we could but remember this marking of the crossroads at each stage of our growth, we would be far less disturbed when we face change. For this recurring mandala is like a bell ringing the turning of days and seasons, calling us to stop and see from whence we have come, saying to us that wherever we go, the entire meaning of existence goes with us. It is unexpectedly important for us to stop sometimes and ask the question, "Where have I come from and how am I progressing?" It is as if we walked about ourselves surveying ourselves from all the possible angles. This patient, periodic circumambulation is, at the personal level, what these fourfold forms of color and light are at the mythic level.

Great stress is placed, in American Indian myths, on these places of centering. Curtin gives a jewel-like example from the Wintu Indians:

Olelbis, the creator, built a great and awesome sweathouse, its middle support being a huge young white oak, with various kinds of oak trees being side supports, various flowering plants serving as binding and as sides. "Then the house began to extend and grow wider and higher, and it became wonderful in size and in splendor. Just as daylight was coming the house was finished and ready. It stood there in the morning dawn, a mountain of beautiful flowers and oak-tree branches; all colors of the world were on it, outside and inside. The tree in the middle was far above the top of the house, and filled with acorns; a few of them had fallen on every side. . . . The sweathouse was placed there to last forever, the largest and most beautiful building in the world, above or below. Nothing like it will ever be built again." [18]

A similar atmosphere and sense of wondrousness is conveyed in the exact words of the Navaho myth in the Haile rendering:

> First Man placed Turquoise in the south, Jet in the north, White Shell in the east, and Abalone in the West, and all these Holy Things grew up and joined together overhead; and he also placed a Red-White Stone north of the east pole and breathed upon them, and a white Hogan rose on these five poles. There were four chambers in the Hogan, and First Man placed in the Hogan floors of Jet, Turquoise, Abalone and White Shell, so the Hogan had four stories in the order named. Everything was created by First Man, who breathed upon the four Holy Materials and they spread out to make the floors. . . . First Man blew east, south, west and north and the building grew larger. . . . First Man enlarged it twice more until there were four circles in the Hogan.

This hogan has four stories, one made of each of the sacred stones. These stones are the wealth of First Man. Thus it is of his very substance that he creates, in the initial barrenness of each succeeding world, the things that mark its uniqueness. The First World of absolute darkness had the rising columns of light and the multicolored columns where the Red-White Stone was. In the Second or Red World, after the light columns rose, the Red-White Stone shook the earth with portents of evil. Now at this prodigal time of the harvest of darkness, here at the midway point of the Third World, once more the Holy Stones are placed. The Red-White Stone is not centered this time, but rests at a northeast point. It is important to note that the Navaho apparently considers the uncompleted circle to be the better one. His dwelling hogan is really an uncompleted circle, with the entrance facing the east. In sandpaintings, snake and rainbow guardians are often shown surrounding the entire painting except for an opening between head and feet (or tail). In the Creation hogan there is an opening between the support at the east and the support at the northeast. From this asymmetrical and unexpected configuration comes the Creation hogan in all its beauty. This is unexpected, as many newnesses are, because here more than at any preceding moment one would have looked for the fifth light column to be in the center of the great hogan-wheel. It is not. Rather it stands between the place of darkness and the place of a fresh arising, as if to signify the responsibility for movement and change and all the dangers therein.

The myth is wiser than we, who adopt a seemingly logical way of action in our "cloud of unknowing." When negativity presses upon us, we are prone to deny our wholeness; when the light is with us, we affirm ourselves. But in the myth, when darkness surrounded the people the mandala form was balanced and centered; at the time of richer creation, unbalanced and fivefold humanness prevails. Similarly, if we want help in avoiding deflation and inflation, we must attend to the opposites in a situation. States of negative self-love and self-hate are results of egocentric one-sidedness, of the hasty assumption that we are identical with what arises in us. We desperately strive to make our Creation hogan perfect. If we could be aware that this cannot be, that whatever emerges from the unconscious areas of our being has continually to be separated from and balanced by conscious attitudes, we would come to a more proportioned sense of our own nature.

Often an outer event or a dream, occurring at a crucial time of either inflation or deflation, serves to restore the needed balance. For example, a man who was becoming rather too proud of the progress of his inner symbols, tending to feel himself personally responsible for their wondrousness, was of a sudden precipitated into a most unpleasant situation with his business partner. Because he had the good sense to see the outer event as largely of his own making, a relative equilibrium could be achived between the outer and inner poles. And it is striking how often a conscious attitude of self-pity or genuine despair is countered by an inner experience of turning up some lost treasure or finding light in an unexpected place. Such happenings as these, if we attend to them with devotion, can carry healing for what Kierkegaard called the "anxiety of presumption" and the "anxiety of humility." [19] They can bring balance to a sense of despair and imbalance to a rigid perfection.

The presence of Coyote in the Creation hogan, and the role he plays there, are quite in keeping with his symbolic meaning as man's tragicomic creatureliness. It was pointed out earlier that Coyote's first appearance marked the end of a totally unconscious innocence in man. In fact, Coyote was seen as the disturbing sense of partialness which haunts man throughout his life. This remains true of Coyote, although new facets of him are now added. When the Holy Ones, First Man and his companions, take their places in the hogan, Coyote's place is assigned on the feminine (north, in this myth) side. But he moves about in the east-northeast opening, finally taking a position by the east pole. He is the wanderer and disturber even more clearly than in the beginning. He stands in the area of imperfection, incompletion. He also contains earth power, feminine consciousness and fertility, thus standing on the side of vegetation, moon, darkness, rather than with the great male gods, or with sun and thunder. That is to say that our state of self-recognition, of separation from the unconscious paradise of the mother womb, does not mean that we can thrust upward unfettered by animal nature. The restlessness present in the Insect People of the lower level has evolved to the restlessness of Coyote as he moves about the place of exits and entrances.

Then, says the myth, "First Man assigned places to all the things to be made for this world, placing them in front of all the people." The primal forms and figures presaging man's wholeness are put more sharply in focus. There is a growing sense of possibility, of potentials not only intimated but already in process. The seed is present in the full corn ears, male and female, white, yellow, blue, striped, variegated. Elements for a fruitful harvest are at hand: earth, rain, clouds, lightning, thunder, darkness, pollen. And amid this splendor and effulgence, in the ever-enriched hogan of Creation, is Coyote, the imperfection which is evolving toward Man.

What is the relationship between any particular individual among us and the eternal presences moving in the myth? Coyote is the archetype of any man's trickster nature. He is *not* the unique individual ego, although in this myth he stands nearest the human, keeping the beauty of realization from being static. This entire scene is a mythic statement of that process by which we become separate and discrete pieces of our world. Symbols are presented from unconscious deeps, including the possibility of our assumption of our own blundering identities. These symbolic presentations—even Coyote—must be consciously realized by us as individual carriers of our own unique life experience. Each of us, the particular men or women relating to a myth by hearing it, reading it, seeing it reenacted, is the framework for the myth. Or at least we can provide the framework.*

* The role of the personal ego (the focal point of the active "I") is often difficult to see in myth and folk tales of the cosmic sort. In the less cosmic folk tales some heroes and heroines can be seen as ego personifications. But cosmic mythological heroes and heroines should not be generally so interpreted. They are generic aspects of man, archetypes of powers and processes. It is we who relate to the myth in various ways—and thus bring ourselves into relationship with it—who constitute the personal egos.

We err by identifying with and being caught up in the affects of the magnificent soul drama; if we fail to bring its archetypes into conscious relationship with our personal lives and circumstances, the unconscious realm rules us and can destroy us. If, on the other hand, the "I" listens or reads with tongue in cheek and a feeling that myths are nonsense, or fails to listen at all—the ego becomes the universe and the inner images are disastrously denied. It is as if some of us are in leaky canoes in a raging sea, some are in luxury liners on a duckpond, and some sail a seaworthy craft on a proper sort of ocean. In relating to myth, whether recorded or subjectively constellated from within or without, we need to bring our personal reality as pilot to guide the craft over the mythic ocean. The individual carrier is not in the myth. The myth is the suprahuman frame of reference for the human work. The developing personality, in its unique aspects, is forming itself within the common mythologem of creation and emergence.

Wonderful though they are, the scenes of the making of the four Medicine pouches which follow the raising of the Creation hogan will, for the purposes of this book, be only mentioned. Because this particular emergence myth places an especially marked emphasis on evil, sorcery, witchcraft, and ways to deal with these, the Medicine pouches contained medicines to counteract evil and to fight against witches. After the four pouches were completed, First Man "distributed among his eight companions . . . all his medicine, good and bad. Witchcraft and the power to cause insanity and evil-wishing were included." Once more we are confronted by the deep and paradoxical truth that the good and the bad, the light and the darkness, are inextricably interwoven in the processes of life and growth.

But as yet there are "no mountains, trees, stones, nor Day, nor Night, nor Sun, nor Moon." Everything needed for a new fertility is present, and still First Man cannot

make the light rise up. What can be missing at such a time
of fulfillment? Who walks unhappily before the new day,
pulling the light back with restless fingers? It is Coyote:
Coyote who has so willingly given of his awkward energy
from the beginning, absorbing his colors from the sacred
columns, telling the meaning of things, letting suffering be
transmitted through him, daring to be the unsettled member
of the house. Why does he object now—or perhaps, more
precisely, to what does he object? Apparently he does not
like being called Wanderer and Scolder. Thus comes again
the inevitable pause in forward motion in order that
another error of growth may be rectified.

This has in it a most necessary object lesson. For us to
use our dim desire to be man, our desire to be free from
the archaic unconsciousness of comfortable containment,
is for us to have to dare humanness and the erring thrust
into danger. Our weaknesses and limitations must be included rather than transcended. Darkness, negativity, evil,
must be incorporated into our sense of self, for we cannot
proceed upward on illusions. It is our own "trickster," our
own Coyote, our own wandering and scolding unholiness
which will help us to know those dark facts hidden from
us by our ideals. When we learn this, if we learn this at
all, we may still have to learn that our unholiness must be
respected; not by a glossing over of its irritable and unpredictable nature, but by an honoring of it in the very
fullness of its imperfection.

Why is this apparently simple act of self-acceptance so
enormously taxing? Because from infancy onward all the
socially collective learning transmitted to us goes in an
opposite direction. We are warned not to be weak, not to
make mistakes, not to admit errors, but to pretend to false
feelings, to strive for perfection. The greater the sense that
this Utopian ideal is unattainable, the more violent is our
effort to achieve it. The walls of defensiveness grow ever
thicker, the human creature more starved in this prison.

It is an act of heroism to begin to break down these barriers brick by brick, as one man actually dreamed he was doing.

> I see a place I know I must reach, but a brick wall blocks my way. I find a rock and start to knock each brick loose. The place beyond is simple but appealing.

This man was faced with "rebirth" into a world of fallibility, ignorance, error, and imperfection—and was being told to stop pretending, to come forth and participate in life just as it was.

Coyote does not wish to be something he is not. He wants only to be respected and to be seen more clearly for what he really is. His essential meaning, behind and beyond the disturbing and the wandering and the scolding, is that of ushering in new consciousness. Wolf and Lion make offerings to him then and address him as He-who-calls-the-dawn and He-who-calls-the-daylight. And he releases the pillars of light, and the "universe functioned again and became holy." And the people can move, in the usual way of the five Holy Stones, up to the next world.

V

Man and Woman

Summary
PLACE OF CROSSING WATERS

This was the Blue World, and better than the preceding ones. There were four mountains in the four sacred colors at the four compass points, and there were valleys and hills and contours on the land. All kinds of earth animals were here, and water animals, and birds of all kinds. There was also the Place of the Crossing Waters, where a north-south stream—placid and cool—passed under an east-west stream—rapid, furious, and warm. And the people were surrounded by water, for the streams also flowed from east to south and west to north. The place where the people emerged into this world was called White-Speck-of-Earth. Animal chiefs had four-storied, four-colored houses at each of the four compass points. These chiefs, two Wolves and two Mountain Lions, at each dawning gave the people instructions as to how they should work and relate. Nadleh, the hermaphrodite, was there, with grindstones, pots, bowls, seeds.

After three years in which the people played, gambled, and labored together, the nine Holy Ones, led by First Man, decided to build another magic hogan, a round hogan. Into this hogan came all the people and seated themselves as before. The Holy Ones brought, in miniature form, all the various sacred stones and jewels. Coyote alone seemed to know the purpose of this ritual and ran about

*telling everyone that male and female genitals were to be
made. Then Coyote said, "No one of you seems to be
able to guess what these things are. I roam about and have
little sense, but I have guessed all of them. You must all pay
great attention to this ceremony since it concerns you all.
This shall be Birth." And all the people contributed, to give
power to the male and female genitalia.*

*Many babies were born, and for four years the people
grew and flourished, with good crops and food stored away.*

"This appeared to be a better world. . . ." The slow
turning movement of change, set in action with the initial
seeking of the Insects in the lowest world, has now reached
a level at the same time fuller, and more humanly real,
than any preceding one. This world at the outset has in it
the actuality of the living substance—mountains, hills, valleys, all kinds of animals, birds, water creatures. A richness
of differentiation clings to this Fourth or Blue World, a
variety of color and form not heretofore visible, or even
possible. In a somewhat oblique manner, the Fourth World
resembles the fifth and sixth days of creation described in
Genesis, where the Lord God created "the great sea monsters and every living creature that moves, with which
the waters swarm . . . and every winged bird" and then
created "the beasts of the earth . . . and everything that
creeps upon the ground." Genesis begins with darkness;
the First World of the Navaho myth also was almost "without form and void." Between the First and Fourth Worlds
—as between the first and the fourth day—lay day and
night, vegetation, sun and moon.

Each Navaho world has begun, explicitly or implicitly,
with a mandala, a fourfold abstract of the total meaning.
Until now these mandalas have been dark fire and light,
ephemeral and shifting. The mandala form in myth and
ritual emphasizes the importance of each stage of the
individuation process as it occurs in a place, a space, uniting
the nowhere with the here-and-now. The unfolding of a

creation myth is like the unrolling of a tapestry on which the "eternal presences" of the collective unconscious are woven into a consciously perceivable and graspable pattern.

Thus it is that this Fourth World begins with two mandala forms each possessing a greater degree of substantiality than those previously initiating a new world stage: an earth mandala of sacred mountains and a water mandala of crossing waters. The four great mountains mark this place as one where the more concrete actualities of human development will move into the center. The presence of hills, valleys, animal life in its many manifestations, bears out the quality of this world. The water mandala—the Place of Crossing Waters or "Waters-flow-across-each-other"—seems to carry in itself not only the possibilities for future differentiation of certain unconscious processes. This water place is not unlike Okeanos of Greek myth, of whom it is said, "Ever since the time when everything originated from him he has continued to flow to the outermost edge of the earth, flowing back upon himself in a circle. The rivers, springs and fountains—indeed, the whole sea—issue continually from his broad, mighty stream." [1] This also recalls the "mighty fount of all waters, a well called Huergelmir," the place in Norse myth from whence all rivers flowed. [2]

In the ancient Chinese *Book of Changes*, [3] the *I Ching*, the "sons" are remarkably similar to the stages of the Navaho myth. The first son is movement and thunder— the restless disturbance of the Navaho beginning world. The second son is danger and water—the difficulties and flux of the Navaho Second and Third Worlds. The third son is the mountain. The youngest, the newest, the least archaic—this is the mountain. This is the upthrust into the realm which is ever closer to the human scene. And this Fourth World at first is interlaced and surrounded by water, although not water in the aspect of either the endless and formless seas of some creation myths, or the later floods. This mandala, this Place of Crossing Waters, is a paradox of structured fluidity, of differentiated flow. One dimension is the east-west river, the dawn-sunset direction encompassing the activity of day, the time of work in the life of primitive man; the other is the north-south river, the midnight-midday current. The first river is the warm and energetic movement of daily reality and consciousness. The second river is the coolness and placidity related to the darkness of the unconscious midnight, to the moon and maternal aspect of the light of the inner world. Together the two rivers form a cross, not unlike the ancient Babylonian solar cross associated with water deities.[4]

And where is this Place of Crossing Waters found in the seeking soul of man? What manner of pivotal point is it on which the new wheel of becoming must turn? As we give ourselves to the terrible and beautiful upward reaching of the spirit, as we struggle to shape and to let be shaped our uniqueness of self, there are recurring places where the small lights of awareness are focused. These are Kierkegaard's "moments," when time and eternity intersect as two streams. We stand, as do the people here, at a White-Speck-of-Earth of emergence, bringing with us all the pain and suffering, the joy and love, which we have felt before. All their meanings flow around us and under us, and we are filled with the sound of them. And we are aware, even if through a mist, of where we have been and of something of what must be done now.

Often, after agonizing months of confusion, anxiety, difficulty, will come a simple dream statement which is like the center of a moving circle. One such experience was that of a woman in her thirties who, after a long and trying time of personal struggle, dreamed that a flood had swept over a small village, almost destroying it. But the waters subsided, and it was found that the statue of the Virgin had survived, with only the robe's hem waterstained. This was her White-Speck-of-Earth with the channeled waters surrounding it. This was a personal statement that the unconscious condition which had existed be-

fore was now altered, that creation was at last being fulfilled, that heaven and nature were being united at a human
level.

After the Fourth World emergence, in keeping with
the more concrete water and earth dimensions, the initial
movements of the myth's characters are also more concrete.
There is a needed structuring and framing of the experience, but neither with the cosmic light columns nor through
the instrumentality of the creator-god, First Man. The
people themselves begin to act, to choose, to work, to play.
Multicolored holiness is not lacking, for each chief's house
has its own particular color sequence based on its own
particular direction. But the sacred colors are related to
those places from which instructions are given about the
labor of each day, about the handling of people. And for
three years the people work creatively together, preparing
the soil, planting, reaping enormous harvests. This is a
new turn in the spiral progression of consciousness, a new
and concretized purposiveness. Man is closer to becoming
man, closer to the sense of being part of a place and a time
and a history.

In contrast to the appealing naturalness of this scene
of the people taking their places in the functional group is
our contemporary era of struggle in a divided sea where
current rages against current, intellect fights instinct, tech-
nology strains for supremacy over nature, scientific speed
crushes spontaneity. Whereas we emphasize masculine one-
sidedness and cultivate only a sparse and sentimental fem-
ininity, the Navaho myth here presents the wonderful
alchemy of earth which combines maleness and femaleness.
The hermaphrodite god, Nadleh, offers his provender:
grindstones, cooking material, seeds. This is the necessary
combination of masculine and feminine in the substance of
man—the seed and the pot, the planting and the grinding.
The pair becomes four, the four become twelve; the seed,
the stones, the flour, and the bread move forward in quiet

succession as Nadleh shows the way toward fruitfulness. The undeniable roots of yet another change are beginning to grope into this earth.

After a period of "settling down" the nine Holy Ones meet and counsel together and decide there should be more creation. "First Man said: 'It will not do to let things go on in this manner. The people are always the same. They have plenty to eat, more than they can use. There ought to be more of them. There should be increase. There should be birth.'" But the new hogan and its miniature mystery seems to be understood by no one except Coyote, who runs about to whisper its meaning to the people. Mark his most unexpected and dramatic words: "No one of you seems to be able to guess what these things are. I roam about and have little sense, but I have guessed all of them. You must all pay great attention to this ceremony since it concerns you all. This shall be Birth." Once more it is Coyote, the lowly, the despised, the restless wanderer, who is able to see what is at hand. Likewise in the myths of several California Indian groups, including Wishosk, Yurok, Karek, and Hupa, the culture-hero-trickster is responsible for the origin of birth.[5]

And the word must now be made flesh; the body must become the container for the spirit. Only individual carriers are able to realize the individuation process, or the centralization of the rhythmic inward life. To be an individual carrier involves a recognition of our own physical nature in all its superb design and its sorry limitations. Every child beginning to be aware of its differences, accumulating experience which leads to a sense of "I," is in process of becoming a conscious carrier of the unconscious mystery. Each of us as an adult, as we repeatedly renew acquaintance with a lost part, is a participant in the same process. The body and sex are basic and living factors in the architecture of the individual carrier, are as intrinsic to the fullness of self-recognition as the mind and the spirit. To forget this, to relegate body and sex to inferior positions in the upward reach of emergence, is to walk certainly into the catastrophe of meaninglessness.

What of body and sex as psychological facts? According to Linda Fierz:

> The body is our first and last outward reality which defines and conditions our life experience and gives us personal identity and continuity. It is our roots, in the earth, the world, in outer life. It is our immediate reality and uniqueness, our first concrete mandala mirroring our peculiarities, and differences. It is the most expressive and faithful burden we have, and we must be kind to it, listen to it. We should be able to bear with our body, especially as we grow older, should deal with it with dignity. We must not project it into complexes and conflicts, but let it be a pure expression of ourselves.[6]

Primitive man has a rich intuitive awareness of the inseparableness of mind and body—an awareness which modern civilized cultures have tragically lost. The bodily foundation of the personality, which functions irrationally and with a debonair disregard for the careful logic of the intellect, cannot be put into a category of nonessential fact, as contemporary man tries so earnestly to do. When the word is made flesh, both flesh and word must celebrate the individual nativity. Emotions and passions are birth pains, moving us forward to a new consciousness in the unconscious. They are not all of life; they are no *final* goal of satisfaction, to be sure. Yet they must be experienced and known. We must be conscious of them; only then can we decide whether to express them outwardly or inwardly, or both. The dual gods, Mawu-Lisa (female-male), of the Fon of Africa are not only seen as cosmic rhythm but by "presenting their two natures alternately to men, the divine pair impress on man the rhythm of life and the two series of complementary elements of which its fabric is woven." [7]

Unless we deal with these elements in an aware way, as Coyote is doing in the myth, a dark and sinister game starts behind our back. Adolescent girls and boys in our Western culture (to the greatest degree in the United States, to lesser degrees in other countries) are being swept into the frenzy of Bacchantes, with substitute ritual objects used for their absurd, dangerous, and pathetic fulfillment. Sport cars, motorcycles, drugs, alcohol, vandalism—these are some of their modes. And their culture permeates that of the "adult" generation, who unfortunately started it in the first place by repression or tawdry expression. Either repression or cheapening of instinctive drives, particularly of the sexual, can only lead to formation of various physical symptoms, to compulsions and addictions, to harmful judgments, and in general to a withering of the personality. These are some of the "dark games" played out when we do not "pay great attention" to this archetype of the Creation of Birth. On the other hand, when we do attend, great things shimmer in the air. (And here also the young generation in the United States is opening the way through such involvements as civil rights works or Peace Corps membership, through its courageous demands for a more humane education and more authentic bases for relationship.)

Do we believe that sacred stones and sacred jewels go into the creation of male and female genitalia? We do not. And why can we not hear the whispered voice of "little sense" in us which relates the miracle of the uniqueness of being? Surely if we are to be in any way a fulfillment of the divine need, we must be so as widely and deeply as possible. God is to be loved with "heart" and "strength," as well as with "soul" and "mind." In a strange shy way, a way too soon snuffed out, children know this. Their own archaic nature mysticism and pantheism is the vision of Coyote, and they see their bodies bathed in the light of a remarkable and unafraid curiosity. We lose this simple wonder which is a kind of reverence as we begin to walk the narrower path of "growing up." Our adolescence, un-marked by puberty rites to dignify our body's self, becomes a confusion and a constraint. Sex becomes an end in itself, albeit a guilt-producing one. We fear ourselves for our impulses and our passions and begin to reject them, slowly losing the awareness that they do "concern" us as whole persons. Only as we become conscious of the split within us, and conscious also of the desire to be one again, spirit and body, word and flesh, joining together in a single community, can we hear Coyote's words: "You must all pay great attention to this ceremony since it concerns you all. This shall be Birth." Then a fuller existence can begin, as it does in the Navaho myth.

Summary

THE SEPARATION

One day, after the eighth year of living at White-Speck-of-Earth by the Place of Crossing Waters, the Wolf Chief of the north arrived home to find his children uncared for, his wife away, his house unattended. When his wife returned, there was a scene, and she refused to do her work. This went on for several days until finally, because the chief was not helping his people, Nadleh the transvestite (hermaphrodite) was called in. He indicated that he had all that was necessary to the men for planting and cooking, and all the men decided to separate themselves from the women and cross over the river.

Four days and nights of consulting among the men followed this decision. During this period they spent the days at the river's edge, the nights at the house of Nadleh. Spider Woman helped to make the house large enough. The third night the chiefs said: "Let us retire and see how our dreams will be." Each morning the rivers had changed colors. The men brought offerings to the Place of Crossing Waters. Eventually they crossed the river, at the Place of Floating Logs, in five wondrous boats, carrying with them all their belongings and all the male children. They were beset by a storm, but Sphinx Moth (Tobacco Horn Worm) calmed the waters, and they arrived at a place called Gathering Shore.

For four years the men prospered; their crops increased; sacred rites of various kinds were established. Meanwhile the women were failing. They had been mating with Fox, Weasel, Badger; eventually both they and the men were pulled into autoerotic excesses.

Now the enormity of being human confronts the people. It is as if, with the Creation of Birth, a new responsibility is laid upon them—an obligation to carry the temporal burdens of the world, including passion and love. Heretofore the people have been more or less passive participants on the cosmic ground of the unconscious, being pushed here and there by the surges of eternal forces in their alignments and shiftings. But in the creation of sexual differentiation, "all the people were to contribute." Different ones brought different bodily elements to create male and female genitalia, and then First Man distributed the created organs so children could be born. In this way, says the myth, "First Man is the source of the evil that did not exist before." After this rite was finished, Coyote said, "We have done well to let new ones come into the world." Evil and good are thus contained in the same act. This is the burden of growing consciousness. When the word is thus made flesh, it is also confronted by mortality, upheaval, sin, and guilt. We face our limitedness and our loneliness. We sin against our limitation by trying to be whole; we sin against wholeness by forgetting to be conscious.

Growth and change seem always to breed upheaval. Most original ideas and revolutions have been condemned by guardians of the old as "sinful." Jesus, Copernicus, Galileo, the Maid of Orleans, Faraday, Madame Curie, Freud, Jung—to name only a few—all were ignored, or accused, or persecuted as heretics, as wanderers from the unquestioned truth. Their "sin" was to reach beyond the contemporary systems. Deep within ourselves a similar war breaks out each time consciousness indicates change. The man trying to find a more real niche for himself gives up his old job and risks disaster by taking another which starts him out lower down the ladder. Friends and inner voices both say, "You fool! No sensible man does this sort of thing. Why not let well enough alone?" The woman who dares to look for creative outlets separate from her family is told she is "reaching for the moon" and has a hard time not believing it herself. In the Navaho legend of Self-teacher,[8] the hero, having come a long and difficult journey with the gods, is left on his own in an untilled wilderness. He thinks to himself that it would have been better had he stayed home where he belonged. Then he adds ruefully, "But I might be dead by now if I had." These are the "sins" and anxieties of commission—sins against inert nature. Consciousness must always pay with this kind of suffering.

Another kind of "sin" and its attendant pains are related not to fulfillment, but to the betrayal of our own integrity of choice. "For what is a man profited," asked Jesus of Nazareth, "if he gain the whole world, and lose or forfeit his own self?"[9] And later he said, "No man, having put his hand to the plough, and looking back, is fit for the Kingdom of God."[10] This backward look, this temptation to forfeit the self, is not a crime against nature, but *for* nature, is a sacrifice of wholeness for the sake of comfort, is a sin of omission. Thus we are "guilty" both for reaching toward the realm of the gods and for betraying our own potential divinity.

In the myth, the first stretch of creation in the Fourth World goes well. For seven years living is good, with flourishing crops and contentment and benevolent leadership. Conflict and creation explode into this scene with the new birth thrust. And it is the same whether in the outer or the inner history of the individual. The archaic containment of childhood is flooded and eroded by the rising tides of adolescent self-awareness. The body becomes an intense and awkward instrument in the life of the spirit, blundering its way outward into the world of irrational emotions. It is not yet supported by the collective consciousness and has no sense of direction or meaning, being impelled at first only by its own animal urges. As individuals held in the body substance, for good or for ill, we may not yet be cognizant of our personal destiny. That destiny is cognizant of us. It reaches for us as the sea reaches for the shore. It surges against us with a powerful love in each rise and fall of our tides, in every error and risk we involve ourselves in. Once the creation of birth is undertaken by the gods, the suffering consciousness of every day is placed in our hands.

Anyone who has ever patiently tamed a wild creature assumes at once a new and more demanding responsibility for it, for blind instincts no longer are sufficient guides. Especially in the area of sex this is so. How soon the naturalness of animals departs from us, and we are expected to guide and control wisely an organism which we have not yet accepted! The public moral code of the United States is a sobering example of irresponsibility toward the psychobiological nature of man. The sentimental and disguised eroticism of the "dramatic" offerings of radio, television, and motion pictures is a poor but widely used substitute for the genuine drama of relationship. The sensitive poetry of the words of love is replaced time and again by the obscene joke. Sex is not to be discussed because it is "bad"—and so a perplexed promiscuity becomes the way people try to reach one another. Mother is glorified into "momism," and as a result men and women alike are caught in an infantile rebellion marked by whispers, giggles, sex play in backseats of autos, and growing cults of "sexual freedom." No one is being responsible for psyche and body as a total and rich unity. Our adolescent emergence is treated like a recalcitrant but unfortunately necessary ass, alternately beaten and doctored.

The wildness of our own adolescence and the wildness of each new inner push are alike difficult, confused, and quarrelsome. To become responsible for them requires much of us. Such a period of trial is now at hand in the myth, when a chief's wife revolts and refuses to do her work of caring for her home and family. Suddenly the masculine/feminine polarity is for the first time brought into sharp focus. It could not have come earlier, inasmuch as the previous differentiations were between larger and more suprapersonal psychic elements. First Woman did, in a vague and generalized way, help First Man. But she was not truly a separately functioning person; and, other than her and the mothering darkness, there has been no woman. Only with the making of sexuality can the male and the female truly be said to confront each other. Then the opposites begin to fall asunder, the tenuous thread of unity breaks, and the separation which must precede real relationship begins.

It is at first a puzzling fact that this myth, coming from a matriarchal people whose dominant orientation is feminine, places full blame for the separation between the sexes on the women. But it is precisely the deep feminine womb, the darkness of the fecund undifferentiated earth-water world, which was the source of what now has come to pass. Even as the first upward way had to be a separation from the primal vessel and a breaking up of this selfsame vessel into many pots, so now man must almost seem to disown the feminine if he is finally to relate to it. The Mother is elementary container without whom no life could be. The Mother is also, however, life-devouring. She is, so it seems, desirous of taking her children back into the darkness from whence she sent them forth. Day passes into night, summer into winter, life into death. If the human being is to proceed as a sentient part of eternal being, he must somehow succeed in getting a foothold in another dimension. Thus cyclic nature, the amoral substance, is blamed for impeding the orderly march of events. Whereas in the beginning

Mother Nature's vegetative prodigality was most evident, at this stage it is her inertia and indifference which loom large.

Wolf Chief says to his wife, "Why have you left the home? Why should you leave the children without food? Isn't it better to provide for them first and then visit with others? I think there are many things to be done about the house in place of running about and doing nothing. It is entirely wrong to leave the children and to neglect them. You should not do these things." She replies, "If you know so well what is to be done, why not do it? You have nothing to do but talk. Take hold of things here and work instead of talking to others all the time! And since you have so much sympathy for your children, you might take care of them instead of speeching and walking around all day!"

Wolf Chief behaves much like an adolescent on the verge of a new maturation. He has lived for eight years in a blissfully unconscious world where the woman cooked his food, kept his house, and bore, nourished, looked after his children. The archetypal Mother contained him without thought. Such an unthinking containment inevitably reaches a saturation point, whether in cultural history or in individual development, and then the shift must be made from matriarchal unconsciousness to patriarchal thrust. For Wolf Chief, the impulsion toward this comes with the shocking recognition that all is *not* well, as he had supposed—that, in fact, he as giver of orders can be insulted, accused of being just a talker and useless. He is literally jolted from his unconscious identification with the unrooted phallic command, even as his wife has been somehow pulled from her unconscious identification with the containing womb. And he must, as the symbolic carrier of the growing consciousness, find in himself and assimilate into himself both masculine and feminine meanings.

It is worthy of note that Navahos, in their words for life stages, have for the stage of babyhood but one name which is neither masculine nor feminine: the "just born," the "newly arrived." Beginning with the stage of "weaning to adolescence," however, each successive life period has two names, a masculine and a feminine one. It is thus clear that the Navahos, too, sense the bisexual polarity as emphasized at puberty. The medium for the start of this transformation in the myth is Nadleh, the hermaphrodite and transvestite who is called "he" and yet identifies himself with woman's work. The chief asks Nadleh, "Have you seeds other than those belonging to women?" He replies that he has all the various kinds of corn, squash, tobacco, and other seeds.

In the development of any of us this phase of conflict and beginning separation should normally come in adolescence, both through actual clashes with parents and through inner awarenesses which shatter the old dependency patterns. Puberty is the time of conflict between approval and independence, between adjustments to the social mores and rising sexual urges. The individualized instincts seem to threaten a virginal freedom and sense of self, and many are the ways we in adolescence try to repress these instincts, to hold them off. We become uncommunicative or sarcastic; we pretend not to care; we get involved in intellectualizing or in antisocial "gangs." One part of us wants to go forward; one wants to hold back. "At every transitional stage of life . . . there is a tendency of the libido to split," [11] and puberty is a most acute stage.

Underneath the often unlovely surface of the bragging boy or the indifferent girl, however, is the lost child desperately trying to be an adult. In the United States (and perhaps in much of western Europe) the physiologically mature adolescent is still treated as a child, is frustrated with regard both to sex drives and to personal social responsibility. Aggression and hostility toward adults is a result. The world is seen as peopled with negative mothers and fathers. If this persists into adulthood, as it so very frequently does, the "grownup" is really still an irritated and irritating adolescent. This phase is often long delayed and must be undergone in our adult years, making it considerably harder. Nonetheless to live out adolescence some way is always essential for any true wholeness and conscious unity of ourselves.

And it is always, as it is in the myth, a painful time of confusion and disorganization and rebellion. What forces the adolescent or the adolescent adult out of the unconscious world is the recognition that life does not mother eternally, but more and more frequently appears to be neglectful and indifferent, to care not at all about maintaining a comfortable orderliness of existence. This apparent difference is not true; but what is really lacking is the adolescent's own responsibility for life and for nurturance through his own efforts. The "other" can no longer be relied on to hold all the instruments of fulfillment. Seed and vessel, grinding and cooking, must be found as substances and processes belonging to oneself. Where this does not happen in adolescence, it happens later.

Every adult, whether man or woman, who is trying to achieve a more conscious balance between masculine and feminine can find in this episode of Wolf Chief and his wife clues for development. The man can learn that, while his rational ordering of his world seems to be proceeding satisfactorily, his feelings and emotions may be forgotten and so may begin to rebel. Perhaps he sleeps when he wants to be awake. Perhaps he gossips rather than works. Perhaps his only communication with wife or children is through irritability and impatience. The woman, too, needs to see what happens when masculine and feminine have no meeting. If, as in the myth, her unconscious and split-off masculine side commands her inner world, she is letting her real womanness be walked over. So she sinks into apathy, or makes chaos out of her relationships, or becomes compulsive about smoking, drinking, sex. For both sexes, therefore, a new discrimination between masculine and feminine is urgent if growth is to continue. Very often men and women are pushed, as are Wolf Chief and his wife, into unexpected ways because the heretofore repressed emotions erupt. The woman may find herself refusing all sexual advances, or being bored beyond endurance by household affairs, or expressing unbridled irritation toward husband and children. The man may wander away from home more frequently, or may spend hours talking of things that really hold no interest for him. In any case, if one or the other tips the carefully preserved balance, thus spilling emotions about in disorder, something must happen, as it does in the myth.

Thus the ceremony of the separation commences. For ceremony it is, as are all mythic stages, containing another level of the transforming mysteries. In keeping with the ritual nature of this ceremony of separation, a new and infinitely more complex mandala emerges. By contrast to the earliest very simple and dimly visible fourfoldness of First World, this one takes the primal directions and the Crossing Waters and adds to these whirling foam and whirling pool of water, floating sticks and floating logs, four chiefs, each chief with twelve people, plus people from the earlier worlds. We are cradled in oblivious oneness; we are wounded and fall asunder; and we reach a new place of awareness—this must be the rhythm of growth. But throughout, the conscious thrust is attended by multiple and varied masculine and feminine components—including First Woman, First Man, Coyote (First Scolder), Salt Woman, and Dark (Fire) God.

Separation from the Mother is not to be undertaken in haste and without preparation. As with any mystery, there is need for contemplation, firm choice, and contact with the inward vision. Four days and four nights are spent by the men and gods at the edge of the waters—days of consulting about and considering the means of transportation to cross the river, nights of restless sleep and dreams in the house of Nadleh. This is the subjective confrontation of that destiny which is an inevitable consequence of discovering the polarized energy of male-female opposition in the psyche. In the process of becoming an individual, this separation from the mother attitude—which attitude can be both a desire to be "mothered" and an unthinking acceptance of things "just as they are"—needs much attention and careful preparing. All spiritual and psychological maturation must be concerned with this stage of shedding the "old man" and of orienting the "new man" to a genuine self-sufficiency. Outreaching consciousness needs to set itself over against seductive unconscious passivity, needs to pull away from the inertia and indifference which is so much a part of the negative feminine. Yet the masculine reach has its negative aspects, too, one of these being the impatient urge to get things done at once. So the urgency must be held back until it is somehow better related to its important task of crossing.

"All has changed and what we saw before has disappeared." So speak the men and gods when they return after the first night to find the crossing streams have taken on the four sacred colors. After the second night the two streams are black and white, sharply and dramatically contrasted opposites. The men spend long hours in making ready magnificent offerings of robes and jewels which are left in the water. Offerings are made to the water itself, so to speak. It is of particular significance that Haile comments about this episode. "(Offerings are now made in this way when the people find themselves terrified by water. The same songs which were sung for this offering are given in the Blessing Rite, and also the same offerings . . . are given to reform a prostitute.)" It seems quite clear from this that such offerings are for the purpose of transforming the devouring or indiscriminate aspect of the feminine into something more disciplined and creative, of making unconscious processes more accessible and understandable. The reference to the curing of prostitutes seems to be an open recognition that lack of proper respect for and relationship to the "water" (the unconscious inner world of charged potential) may result in misuse of energy, sexual and nonsexual.

Many sexual problems arise because unconscious processes have not been dealt with. A childish woman, clinging and anxious, does not arouse mature erotic responses. Nor does a childish and irresponsible vagabond of a man. Both types may fall into "prostitution"—in the sense of misuse of energy through autoerotic practices or through a too easy sexual submission to another. There are other patterns, too, as, for example, the woman who feels that to have sexual intercourse with a man is to bestow on him an invaluable gift, or the man who believes his sexual prowess is his measure of worldly success. None of these patterns of behavior could continue on their destructive and egocentric way if their possessors were mindful of the deeper processes of growth. Certainly part of anyone's reluctance to open himself to his unconscious world is based on a partially justified fear that it may swallow him. It may do just that; and it has, particularly when he plunges in recklessly without any real awareness of the power of unconscious energies, or is not armed with the proper talisman for the safe crossing, as were the men trying to separate themselves from the women.

More precisely, what is the nature of the feminine principle at this stage of the emergence? It is of enormous importance to be as clear as possible in distinguishing the many aspects of such archetypal manifestations; otherwise we lose ourselves in marshes of vagueness where everything is merged into everything else. Let us recapitulate. Mother-night-and-nature was the place of the beginning. This is the feminine as container, the primal source of sprouting and germinating, the ripe earth whose future crop is as yet undefined. Even as each seed must grasp for itself its own small parcel of soil if it is to have independent life, so each separate part of the developing individual organism must find its unique rooting ground in the generalized psyche. A kind of psychological mitosis ensues, wherein the undifferentiated "egg" of the Mother begins to change. Pot Carrier remembered and fetched his pots—and the great benign container is fragmented into many small containers. Thus Mother-night-and-nature is no longer the encompassing totality, although her substance is carried on the painful upward climb. Such fragmentation, although it may seem chaotic or unmanageable to the individual in whom it occurs, is a necessary step in differentiation. The unity of the egg becomes a complex multiplicity. The softness of the infant changes into the more difficult ego demand of the child. Personality loses its cornerless pliability and moves into a world of alternatives and choices. All this does not mean, however, that life force can or does prosper through an unmitigated and naked thrust forward. While a bold "masculine" courage is what helps us to risk the new and strange situation, the awkward action, it is a down-to-earth "feminine" facing of things as they are which lets us stay in the strange and the awkward with some degree of willingness.

From the myth's early scenes until the time of the separation, feminine figures in any clear delineation are very few. Aside from incidental references, only First Woman and Salt Woman are momentarily singled out for mention. It would appear that, following the early breakup of the Mother-container, the psychological task must for some time be the unremitting work of exploration and expansion, the struggle for increasing light in the unconscious. The paradox is that although the initial departure occurs very early, nonetheless a long sequence of upward progressions remains almost entirely within the unconscious mother realm. First Woman is the early, undifferentiated feminine "mother" in a mythic sense, but not Mother-night-and-nature. When the men depart for the farther shore, she goes with them. Salt Woman never appears as mother in any sense. She is, rather, the imaginative awareness of necessity. She is a visible symbol of the substance, the necessary biological substratum of the spirit.

One could say, therefore, that the feminine as unconscious container is replaced by, or transformed into, the feminine as the substance on which the developing consciousness stands and grows taller. Moreover, when male and female genitalia were made, in the Creation of Birth ceremony, a new aspect, the feminine as opponent, began to emerge. That is, Wolf Chief's wife as representative of the opposing feminine, standing against Wolf Chief as masculine leader, sharpens the consciousness of both the men and the women by making her demands. The newly constellated psychological tension-opposition really arises because the feminine is caught between conflicting desires: the desire to be more conscious, and the desire to stay unconscious and to pull back everything which has achieved some degree of light.

This tug of war can be seen at several levels. It may be found as a struggle within the woman's psyche, or within the man's psyche, or as a conflict between a man and a woman. An individual woman experiences this tension-opposition as the pull of her deep need for heightened consciousness on the one hand and, on the other hand, her natural inclination to remain an unconscious container for the man. It is generally easier—in the sense of more comfortable—for a woman to let Mother-night-and-nature carry her whole meaning. Thus she plays out the ancient roles of mistress, wife, comforter, mother, with little or no concern for whatever uniqueness she may have as a *person*. She is generic Woman, indistinguishable, unspecified. Once she begins to ask, "Who am *I*?" her inner oceanic equilibrium is upset, she is at war within herself, the "separation" has begun. Her creative masculine aspect is shocked, as Wolf Chief was shocked, into a clearer appraisal of her total situation and what is necessary for completion.

The individual man, as long as the tension-opposition is inward, is torn between the downward pull of the Mother with her sedative and deceptively cradling effect and the growing urgency of his masculine need for discriminations and differences. The feminine side of him often tends to "dissolve the ego and consciousness in the unconscious," [12] leaving the man in bondage to the mother. What the men of the myth, led by Wolf Chief, seem to be doing is trying to free themselves from dissolution in feminine negativity. They are propelled into the separation by the active hostility of the feminine.

This "battle of the sexes," seen at the level of actual man-woman relationship rather than as an entirely inward event, is somewhat different. In the myth, the men are forced to action by the wife who refused to be mother-wife any longer. The woman's inner masculine purposive thrust becomes aggressive and forces the man to confront and be more conscious about his inner feminine relatedness. Fortunately for the evolution of the human being, men and women are often drawn into such situations.

A man is reasonable, and reasonably contented, so long as a woman carries the burden of relationship. But the woman begins to feel restless and incomplete, as if something in her wanted her to be conscious of her consciousness. Like Wolf Chief's wife, she is apt to wander off on ventures of her own and, when reprimanded, may retort that the man had better not talk so much, had better take care of his children himself. At this juncture, the man's resentment can lead him, too, to take action regarding relationship, even if at first such action may be divisive. Sexual harmony based on old taken-for-granted premises falls into disharmony. Release of sexual tension either proves to be no release of any deeper tension or becomes impossible until better conscious relationship is worked out. All manner of situations, from the discipline of children to the choice of profession, come under scrutiny and argumentative evaluation. And for both the man and the woman, this clash of opposites, if met with courage, may lead through suffering to transformation.

How does the change go forward in the myth? The

men make their offerings to the water, and that very night
the four chiefs have important dreams. Each chief dreams
that he is standing in a different element: White Corn,
Evening Twilight, Still Waters, Child of Water. It is as
if the collective dreams are saying to the men that now,
with life fertility in their hands, they are ready to go down
into the waters, into the night leading toward a fresh
awakening. (The corn is male, related to White-corn-boy;
Evening Twilight and Still Waters surely make a quiet
downward movement; and Child of Water is another name
for the introverted and more "feminine" of the male Navaho
twin war heroes.) And the next day the river is even in
color and flows smoothly. They begin building boats for
their crossing, five boats of willow and cottonwood,
decorated with water plants, supported by rainbows, sun
rays, and other light elements. They collect all the male
children, together with "all their belongings, the fire of the
Fire God, the stones of the Otter, the wood of the Beaver,
the salt of the Salt Man and all their waterpots and utensils."

The final dramatic scene of the action of separation is
the launching of the boats. This scene is drawn in the vivid
lines of the changing dawn-to-darkness sequence so familiar
in Navaho myth, replete with the numinous abstract sacred
colors and forms. Godlike earth and water creatures—
Horned Toad, Beaver, Otter, Green Frog, Tadpole—act
as the guides and guardians. As the five boats set forth on
the waters, however, no amount of cosmic armaments can
prevent the rising of threatening waves and water monsters.
Any such transitus, it must be remembered, is perilous—
which is precisely why we must wait, observe, dream, and
in all possible ways relate to the meaning of the transforming imperatives. No child's play, this, but a task demanding
a great degree of courage, preparation, and readiness to
face the unknown event.

What is trustworthy in a time of storm is often
strangely small; for example, Tobacco Horn Worm, who
"said he could drive off these monsters." As was seen

earlier, in the first episodes of Second World, the god in the small frequently enters in when there is a temptation to make the too fast, too large leap into newness. Diminutive gods have healing and mana power in their apparent limitedness. American Indian myths have a number of such beings. The Navahos tell of Dontso, the Messenger Fly, and Spirit Wind, as well as Sphinx Moth. Curtin relates the story of the tiny boy, dug up where "little piles of fine soil are brought to the surface by earthworms." [13] This little one became a divinity. The Wintun Indians have a deity described as a tiny person about the size of a thumb. All the "thumblings" of European folk tales belong in the same general category.

A modern example of just such a crucial "crossing," and the role of the small in it, is the following dream of a woman who was confronted with the risky change from a too rational outlook to one of greater wholeness:

> I am plunged into a rough sea where the waves are very high. I am afraid that I will drown, and I try to get someone to help me but cannot. Then I see a woman's apron in the water, and in its pocket I find a thimble. As I hold this, I know I will be all right.

Up to this point in her life, she had relied almost entirely on reason and intellect to carry her along. She was afraid of emotions lest they engulf her as they had engulfed her mother, an irrational hysterical invalid. But the woman's dream-myth reassured her that she would be safe in the rough unknown seas ahead if she let herself find and explore the small feminine values, homely and prosaic as aprons and thimbles.

Small voice, small thimble, small caterpillar—these are things to make the winds and waves subside. And the boats arrive at the opposite side, and this is "a very smooth and lovely place and they called it the glittering shore; the river cast upon the bank there the holy jewels; White Shell, Turquoise, Abalone and Jet. Also the river cast up Red Shell and Pollen, and the people named places there after these jewels." If it is true that this crossing marks a difficult creative thrust of the growing and awkward ego consciousness, then it should be marked by the numbers and symbols of imperfection and creatureliness. Thus there are five boats, not four; and in those boats are not only the riches for a future wholeness but also the needed equipment for individual work as well as all the evils of the previous worlds. The glittering shore of the life river is a place of possibility, not perfection.

So the men set about establishing a new order. Led by Nadleh the hermaphrodite, they plant corn in twelve circles beginning in the east, each planting his own seed; and they make a square farm, planting it in a sunwise direction. Some take on women's tasks of grinding, cooking, feeding the children. For three years the farms of the men increase and prosper, while the women, on their side of the river, are wasting their substance and becoming impoverished and exhausted.

The opposites have virtually fallen asunder. Insofar as this episode may reflect a development of cultural consciousness, the separation could well represent the domestication of the hunter, the assimilation by the tribal masculinity of certain needed survival abilities such as sewing, planting, child rearing, grinding. The behavior of the women, in such an interpretation, would be the insistent pull toward irresponsibility. The same story of the separation, viewed as an archetypal manifestation, has a somewhat similar, yet a somewhat different, meaning. The masculine, as already indicated, has been reaching outward, thrusting forward since the first restless movements. But a principle of distinction, of differentiation, is necessary if the masculine outreach is not to become an overreach. In this sense, "domestication" of the hunting consciousness is imperative not only for primitive man but for modern man. This involves the interpenetration of outward action and inward feeling: in the myth the men learn the women's tasks, aided by Nadleh. The women, who are misusing their powers and becoming thereby impoverished, are then as an archetypal symbol the negative feminine cut off from creative purpose. Anyone, man or woman, who has had experience with this heavy purposelessness—autoerotic, self-pitying, and self-indulgent—knows what the negative feminine principle can do.

Necessary as the separation into opposites is, however, there comes a time when the sundering reaches its limits and the alternatives are seen to be either complete dissolution or relationship on a new basis. Each movement of growth has its own particular ebb and flow, its shifting of the alignments of forces. These cannot be arrested. They can only be felt into, responded to, worked with. To forsake the comfortable mother-womb and walk into the exposed land of separateness, where reward and responsibility are inextricably linked, is one of the hardest tasks put upon man. It gives an exhilarating sense of accomplishment when the Glittering Shore is reached, and living is enriched and vitalized. Yet with it come added trials and frustrations, calling for still more comprehensive awareness. The people in the myth are caught in the web of their chosen destiny now, with the work of conscious reconciliation demanded of them if the masculine and feminine are not to be forever split apart.

Summary

SACRIFICE AND RELATIONSHIP

Nine times of planting and nine times of harvest passed. The women became more and more wretched. They mated with animals and engaged in many sexual excesses. Some of the men, too, defiled themselves with animals. One of them was shattered by lightning because of this and had to be revived and restored by a ceremony which included the divine helpers—Dark God, the hero-twins—and Gila Monsters who "find things by feeling."

Finally some of the women in desperation tried to swim the river. A few were drowned. Wolf Chief called to his wife, "Do you really want to cross?" She replied, "I beg of you to bring us back." The women were brought across the river and a series of purification ceremonies held for them. Owl, Squirrel, Toad, and Frog directed the cleansing. Marsh Wren Woman and Snowbird Woman got bowls of jewels and dew from Pot Carrier, helping thus to sweeten and finally to purify the women. And the women moved into the houses of the new village.

BOTH the men and the women have fallen into sexual indulgences and excesses because of the long separation, and both groups are thus being exhausted. When the two halves of masculine/feminine, or spirit/substance, are too widely pulled asunder in the psyche, too much of something usually appears. Excess is one symptom of the chasm between the opposites of masculine and feminine. There comes to be a one-sidedness of personality where a stronger side compensates for a weaker, just as a man walking the deck of a tilting ship tilts himself in the opposite direction. The overload may be on the side of intellect or emotion, of rational ideas or irrational acts, of aggressive busy-ness or antisocial withdrawal; but in any case it is marked by the symptom of excessive affects such as anxiety, fear, rage, passion. It is as if the psychic energy in its healthy state circulated freely between the demands of consciousness and the needs of the unconscious, between spiritual possibility and substantial necessity. In an unhealthy state, a condition of split, all the energy is, as it were, caught in a too small place with no circulation possible, and all it can do then is build up pressure and explode. Precisely this is occurring in the myth.

Some beginning must be made toward relieving the pressures. The men initiate the creative steps of restoration of balance, as could be expected. It must be the striving masculine which first sees and admits partialness and error, just as it had to be the conscious masculine principle which rightfully carried out the earlier separation; otherwise healing might be merely a passive falling back into the primal mother world. In fact, the first awareness of the need to alter the situation comes to the men when one of them, because of his excesses, is struck by lightning and killed, then disappears.

Perhaps always the new step is taken only as the support of social collectivity is lost, as one is beset by aloneness and separation. The emphasis is changed, and there is a "fall" from that unity of awareness which heretofore has seemed secure in its productivity. Until now the men in the myth have fared very well and have adequately maintained their world without their opposites. The masculine principle of growth, the urgent sense of purpose, for quite a time can thrust ahead and not suffer thereby; but when an extreme position of one-sidedness is reached, a new balance needs to be found.

This is as true for the woman as for the man, though the manifestations of each sort of one-sidedness will be different. The man may remain entirely unconscious of his feminine principle and only live it through projections on outer women, thus never really relating individually to any woman. The woman, likewise, unaware of her masculine principle, may seek its fulfillment in unconscious and unindividual projections. When the feminine is very little projected—that is to say, is allowed to dominate the interior world in larger or smaller degrees—the man is apt to become moody, sullen, childish, petulant, even lethargic. A woman ruled by an unconscious masculine may be dominating, judgmental, autocratic, hyperactive. Each sex needs eventually to be conscious of and to learn to use more creatively the contrasexual principle within; then real outer relationship can be achieved. But this can only happen first through projection, then through the withdrawal of projection (or "separation"), then through discouraging regressions which often follow, and finally through the reuniting. For example, in this myth when the men try to get along without the women in *all* ways, including the erotic, they are forced to revert to a lesser level of adaptation. Animal drives replace relationship, and a shattering, a dismemberment, is inevitable. So the thunder sounds, and deadly lightning becomes the master for the time being.

Thunder gods and "shattering" are well-known mythological motifs. In Egyptian myth, Seth is said to be the "thunderer," the "destroyer." Zeus frequently used his thunderbolts to punish erring gods or heroes. Thor was the redheaded god of thunder.[14] The South American Indians bowed before Huracan, the "mighty wind." Bayley believes the bull-roarer, widely used in the past (even in Greek mystery cults) and still employed by various "primitive" groups today, is related to wind, spirit, and thunder. Thunder is felt to be the voice of the god.[15] The protagonist of another Navaho myth, the Hail Chant, is destroyed by lightning and only with great difficulty is his body reassembled and re-enlivened. Many are the heroes who are "shattered." Tammuz, Attis, Adonis, Dionysus, Balder— all are killed in violent ways. Does this not mean that whenever some part of the universe, whether within the psyche or in society, reaches a heroic size and threatens to become overblown, disproportionate, it must topple or be toppled?

Every human life lived in a more than animal fashion is faced with recurrent shatterings such as these. Development does not proceed uniformly, but by climbs and falls, assemblings and disruptions, births, deaths, and rebirths. Whenever an extreme of fullness is reached, individuation pushes ahead by means of chaos and darkness. In the Chinese *Book of Changes,* the hexagram "Executioner" [16] has as its image "distress or exhaustion." The judgment indicates that to have all one wants means psychological distress. Moreover, says the hexagram, "it is profitable to make sacrifices," and this leads to happiness. Consciousness as a process of becoming more whole must involve the push upward and forward, the separation of one part from another, the resultant partialness that collapses under its own weight, guilt and sacrifice, then a fresh upward step. And the climb out of darkness is accomplished only if we stop to see what has happened, assume full responsibility for it, and willingly take whatever action is needed to correct it.

So the man who is shattered by lightning and is lost becomes the symbol of the "fall" of the masculine thrust. He must be found. The masculine principle must learn to "know" in the sense of the noncanonical statement, "Man, if thou knowest what thou doest, thou art blessed." A reversal of direction, a religious ritual descent, is the way to knowledge.

Aided by the gods, the men discover their lost member below the waters in the abode of Smooth Thunder. The Black God of Fire—he who represents the intense vision to be found in aloneness—is precisely the one who can safely go into the deep and recover the lost. After the men have spent an anxious and sleepless night, they ask Black God if he can help. "To be sure I can," he answers. "I have been waiting all this while to be asked." He goes then to the underwater home of Smooth Thunder to request the return of the lost. Thunder refuses. Black God sets fire to the waters and only extinguishes the fire when Thunder gives songs and frees the man. In this cosmic contest with Smooth Thunder, Dark God uses the ancient alchemical solvent of "burning water"—the alkahest—to redeem the missing man. He also participates in an exchange of sacred songs so that both provinces are enriched. In the inner world of myth and dream that aspect of the "archai" (eternal presences) embodied in such figures as Black or Dark God really stands for higher levels of consciousness. Dark God is the light in the depths of the unconscious, and as such he enables the whole company to have a greater sense of what lies ahead. Thus he can bring about a freer relation to the lower realm by getting Smooth Thunder to cooperate.

The awesome inward experience of the "light shining in the darkness" is the ultimate meaning of the black gods. The veil never quite lifts from their faces, and man can never be quite sure of their intent. For the dark gods, intent is shrouded in paradox. In the Hypnerotomachia,[17] the figure of the black king has under it the inscriptions "Seek and thou shalt find" and also "Leave me alone." Such a paradox can and must be encompassed by man as a way out of the unconscious suffering of choiceless existence. The dark gods help man to seek and find the lost by prodding man to know himself in his allness, not his partialness; but man must never delude himself that he *is* a dark god. Hence the injunction, "Leave me alone." Hence also the reluctant behavior of the Navaho Dark God in crisis situations, where he must be both left alone and at the same time persuaded, for he has been waiting to be called.

Another aspect of the male principle comes through the Gila Monsters, who "find things by feeling and are called Rough Men." They, like Dark God, help to find elements lost by excesses. The power of darkness, the strength of rough feelings—both add a dimension to that masculine striving which so easily falls prey to the lure of light.

How certainly this is a true portrayal of what is happening in many parts of the modern world! A mighty fortress of light has been erected on the foundations of science and rational thought—a fortress from which warm feminine containment and relationship have been separated. Isolation and fear lie just below the surface; yet even two world wars and the continual threat of a third (as well as continual "smaller" ones) have not yet brought us to the place of recognition. We have not yet really seen the imminent "fall," have not acknowledged our littleness, have not let Dark God and Gila Monster give assistance. From a psychological-religious point of view, each of us stands in the midst of a crumbling civilization and can salvage it only by finding in ourselves the missing man and performing over him the songs, prayers, and rituals of untying and renewing.

This is the time of sacrifice and giving over. Dark God gives to Smooth Thunder, and Smooth Thunder gives to Dark God, so each one sacrifices a certain autonomy. Smooth Thunder is the punisher; he is that of God in the unconscious which disciplines the inattentive spirit. Dark God is the helpful divinity, concealed but available, ready to use his redemptive fire when asked. In their exchange of songs they become part of each other; and man must deal with both of them, and be dealt with by both, before he can go free. Together they begin to delineate the "living God" whose presence is awesome and into whose hands it is a "terrible thing" to fall. In the elaborate and beautiful ceremonies following the finding of the lost, many offerings are made to the Holy Ones. Rigidity, arrogance, self-determination—all must be renounced. Rituals such as the untying of knots and the passing through hoops require a humble admission of tension and sterility and of the need for rebirth.

While the men are beginning to cope with their own chaos, the women are voicing their sense of incompleteness by trying to swim the divisive river. Many are drowned. The rest are starving and wretched. This is another portrayal of the distress of partialness which must be faced if relationship is to be achieved either within oneself or between oneself and the other. Every man and every woman can come to know where one-sidedness resides, can see where the deepest affections stir below the surface of life. Outer events or inner happenings push toward the separation, the parting of the road where the paths disappear into shadows and anxious obscurity. One can at that moment follow the way of healing, which is to stay with the aloneness and the hunger and the fear until excess forces change. Another way, tragically chosen too often by modern man, is to ignore the existence of incompleteness and to let the creative substance burn itself out in futile attempts of parts to fulfill the destiny of the whole. This is manifested in the increased straining after power, whether on highways or in places of learning, the increased use of alcohol and drugs, the emphasis on "success" as the criterion of a full life. The conflict is muted, forgotten; the potential growth inherent in conflict atrophies and dies.

This is not the path followed in the myth. Here there is a positive solution because from the beginning the central concern has been with growth rather than adjustment. Had the early restless insect beings settled for adjustment, the primal mother world would have held them forever. The groping outward and upward in the dark unknown, however, has kept alive the roots and tendrils of the plant of becoming. Consciousness in striving for life has, to be sure, led to evil and separation and shattering, but it is still purposive and will not let itself crystallize into a set form. The masculine element of logos, the father world, has recognized its lacks and errors and has ritually worked at sacrifice and purification. Now it is time for the male purposiveness and meaning to consider what has become of the female substance so necessary to its ongoingness.

As one person said, "I've always had pretty good ideas, I guess. But now I realize that they aren't any help to me unless I use them on the facts of my daily life." Not only must we have insights about new ways to approach our situation but we must put them to work. For no sun can quicken to life an earth which is barren, and no plow can turn furrows in a nonexistent field.

So after the men plant and harvest for the ninth time, as the days begin to shorten and the autumn nights to grow colder, the men decide to help the women to return.

> One chief said: "The time for reconciliation is at hand. Whatever their feelings may have been in the past, we should hold out no longer, my brethren!" The four chiefs agreed that it was time to make peace, and they said to the Hermaphrodite, "Tell the people to stay at home tomorrow and not go to work."

Once again the hermaphrodite god serves as mediator, as objective feeling in a time of need. The terrible plight of the women seems to show how profoundly the feminine principle has fallen into its own negative animal side. The women are weak, hungry, dirty, ragged, and foul-smelling. When they first arrive across the river, they are put in a corral like animals. Owl covers them with Darkness, and they are fed. Here the women represent Mother-night-and-nature in one of her most bestial and repulsive guises. All animal, earth, night qualities, it is evident, belong to the feminine at this point. But the beginning of transformation comes through higher feminine preforms—Owl and Darkness.

In the terrible and beautifully poignant Greek myth of the loss of Persephone-Kore to the subterranean places, it is the sorrowing mother Demeter in her dark aspect, and the helpful Hecate, who work for the redemption of the maiden. Like soft feathers of the night-roaming owl, the benign mother must cover the naked incompleteness of errant children until they are fledged anew. In the Navaho myth creatures of earth serve as handmaidens. Things of the earth purify and restore the soul. Even the bowls of Pot Carrier, the Beetle who remembered to include the creaturely mother from the dark beginning, are used to provide the "smell of jewels" mixed with dew brought by Marsh Wren Woman to the women.

Like all archetypal preforms of man's wholeness, the mother principle, too, ebbs and flows, is positive, negative, positive—depending on man's stage of progression on the journey. So here the mother returns—as Marsh Wren, dew, the smell of jewels, even perhaps as the first faint expression of love and need. She is no longer the earliest primal mother of the beginnings, nor is she to remain the bestial negative mother. She is now slowly becoming a greater softness and sweetness, a genuine effort to relate, to bring things together again. It is a joyful time when someone who has struggled and suffered through the ordeal of sacrificing the neurotic demands and the old irresponsibilities is able to say, "I feel more at home, more at peace"; or when someone who, having been all but consumed by a cruel parent, has resolutely rejected all relationship, first reaches out in a shy expression of love.

What deep need there is for new ways to mark life's profound moments! This long sequence of separation, loss, sacrifice, and rerelationship is luminous with ritual passages and the creation of "mysteries." A sweat house helps the men to cope with extreme fatigue after their third year of separation. At about the same period, too, come the colorful rituals for the corn harvest, during which the rustling of the corn and the sound of the voices of Corn People in the night seem to shake the field. Rites for hunting, and hunting songs of various kinds, help the finding of game. For the men lost through their excesses, elaborate ceremonies are held for purification and healing. Finally, when the women return, the mysteries of earth and sweat, of toads, frogs, marsh wrens, snowbirds, all combine to set right what has been divided and wrong.

Even as the tolling of bells marks the crossing of time into eternity, so participation in ritual mysteries marks the merging of meaning with seemingly fortuitous life events. The sense of mystery thus becomes, as Schmitt has said, "an expression of something mightier than the human, an expression of the 'sensus numinus.' "[18] Such expressions of mystery, incorporated into ritual acts, seem to be essential for a final understanding of the nature of changelessness and change; because the need to unify and separate and unify again leads to the enunciation of rhythm itself as a meaningful mystery.

For example, the Shilluk peoples of Africa believe that the great coordinator, Nyikang, both unifies and differentiates, separates, individuates, and orders relationships.[19] And is this not the role of ritual mysteries? In our time, to be sure, the "dromenon has traveled inward," [20] and the mystery is evoked through dreams and psychotherapy, through the arts, sometimes through religion and the church. One way or another, man needs to celebrate his becoming. Not only birth, marriage, and death are peaks in a cycle, but so is each time of transition or confusion, of pain or progress, of desolation or fullness. These are all points of purpose. Each should be gathered into the circle of a life with songs and prayers, with sweat house and celebration, so that no possible meaning shall be left unhonored. The known reach of man's maturity is small enough at best and does not need the added constriction of disregard. On the other hand, the stretch of man's spirit is infinitely great, worthy of whatever beauty of symbol and ritual can be given to it.

VI

Consummation

Summary

FORM AND FLOOD

Despite the reconciliation between the men and women, all did not go well. Some of the people began having bad dreams. Also, First Man punished some of the men who had been practicing witchcraft, adultery, and the like, by causing them to itch and swell. Many weeds came up amid the crops. Some people went crazy. Eagle Man provided medicines for healing. Four Dontsos, Messenger Flies, also helped to heal.

Then Coyote appeared, running about and being troublesome. He was pursued, shot at, finally wounded by the hunter's arrows. Now a child was heard crying near Floating-Water place. Attempts to find it proved fruitless. Dreams were reported, telling that Holy Girl had illegitimately borne a shapeless, black, gourdlike egg. After four days, this egg broke open; two boys emerged, grew up, and disappeared.

Coyote found another baby at Floating-Water, wrapped it in sunlight, and carried it away. Floods began, the waters rose, and the people feared. The two boys born of the gourd-egg returned with tall reeds, and the people went into these to escape the rising floods. Finally, with the help of Locust, the people learned that Coyote had stolen the baby and that this caused the flood. Coyote relented, and the "child fell from the place where Coyote had hidden him

*near his heart, and Coyote also exhaled the child's cry that
he had swallowed. First Man put an offering into the flood
and then placed the child in it, and water ceased to flow
upward."*

*Badger, Locust, Mountain Sheep People, made a hole for
emergence into the next world, but it filled with water and
monsters. Spider Woman and Spider Ant made colored
webs to hold the waters back. After four days waters and
monsters both subsided, Winds helped to dry out the world,
and the people climbed up to it.*

THROUGH all the arduous and labyrinthine journey the
beings and gods have struggled to reach ever fuller realization and comprehension. The fecund feminine womb container, Mother-night-and-nature, benign and rich with unknown life in the beginning, repeatedly has exerted her
deathly backward pull. Struggles for consciousness have
been many, showing clearly how great must be the urge for
spiritual progression if it is to overcome the enormous
weight of primeval darkness.

This eternal battle in the psyche is there for modern man
just as surely as for primitive man, because the law of
psychological gravity is on the side of substance and nature.
This is why we must be repeatedly reminded. Mothering
darkness is, first of all, the shelter within which life is
conceived, held, and nurtured, as it was evidenced in the
early scenes of this myth. It is warm with possibility,
seductive with dreams of what might be; but no responsibility attaches to this aspect of the mother principle. Only
as the initial undirected desire for identity is felt and
acted upon does the positive father thrust begin to emerge.
And at this stage the mother shows her claws. The great
She will not loose her children easily or willingly. Pot
Carrier forgets his pots, "evil" is repeatedly a plague to the
people, the sacred upreaching columns are rendered immovable, the Feline People (basically an aspect of the
feminine moon and night archetype) set themselves against

the emergent beings, the women refuse to cooperate with the men in the making of a new life. Thus the original Good Mother becomes the Devouring Mother, the negative Witch, when her dark, sweet kingdom is threatened. Not that this is the feminine principle in its entirety. But until the rebirth direction is firmly and courageously affirmed and followed, the mother does not give of her higher powers and life-providing nurturance. Although at this point in the myth the women have returned, the mother is not yet functioning at a new level.

Here the people must be viewed in the light of their unremitting efforts to achieve some degree of independence of consciousness. They have arrived at a place of tentative balance, of opposites sundered, discriminated, and reunited.[1] They are taking up their existence where it was left before the separation. The differences are that the women, having been caught at an animal level, and the men, having tested themselves in the more personal feminine spheres of planting, grinding, cooking, are both ready for a new phase. The men now resume their hunting role, while the women welcome the men and "put the houses in order." It is noteworthy that the women also take charge of the medicine bundles of the men. That is to say, the magic remains in—or returns to—the domain of the feminine, the unconscious world where the reconciling symbols are born and are eternally contained.

Almost at once stirrings of a renewed pressure come in the form of bad dreams about Whirling Winds and disturbing signs of sky streaks in the sacred colors. Static balance is not the optimum condition for growth, and growth most assuredly is going on because the eleventh crop is being planted. Evidence that this planting is at a more advanced level is found in the fact that a planting stick is mentioned for the first time.

The planting stick, enabling holes for seeds to be made with less effort than previously, marks a forward step in the primitive agricultural techniques and thus a forward step in cultural consciousness. When man begins to till the soil, rather than merely to gather the fruits of nature's generosity or frugality, he is putting responsibility for existence much more under the aegis of his own ego. He can say, "*I* will plant *my* field," and mean by it that he and nature, the gods or God, are working together. A child's "I" is his first planting stick, his first sense of having an identity of his own. So also is an individual's every step which makes him more the planter of his soul's ground. And this grasping of ego awareness in not an easy achievement because, while it gives us a real sense of belonging to ourselves, it also gives responsibility for errors as well as for accomplishments.

Presumably the bad dreams and signs are related to the events of the time of separation, inasmuch as the myth tell that, while the men were planting, "First Man had dropped mixed stings into the food; these were given them because they had been practicing witchcraft, adultery, etc., and when the people who had been sinful had eaten, they began to itch and they scratched all night and swelled up and were covered with blood." Thus begins an agonizing period of painful sicknesses. Whereas before misfortune has come as injury or death from *outside* or from suprapersonal forces, here it comes from *within* the person.

The unconscious individual sees his difficulties as arising from outside himself, and only as he becomes more conscious does he recognize the genesis as an inner one. The psyche of man is composed of manifold and varied parts, each having its own particular contribution to make to the prospective wholeness. That which we call "I" is generally, except in infants and psychotics, the most clearly defined and "known." As to other parts, they struggle along relatively "unhonored and unsung" until some constellation of outer or inner events forces recognition of them. It is very much as if that which was destined to become a democracy began and remained for a long time a dictatorship where all unorthodox and unfamiliar objects were at once clapped into prisons or concentration camps, or were otherwise outlawed. In a political system, this of course gives rise to innumerable "scapegoats" to be blamed for all sin and error and so to carry the burdens of the society's incompleteness.

The formation of personality, the journey to the self, is not far different. At first there is anarchy of a sort. Then, as the "I" or ego strengthens, a dictatorship emerges where all the negative, difficult, unorthodox, fallible elements are banished, one by one, into unconsciousness. And whatever evidence of these poor prisoners may be found by the "I," it is put into the "others" outside, who are made to carry the buried sense of incompleteness. So long as this condition lasts, there will be unhappiness in the ego-I and seething upheaval within. Constructive change is at hand when the ego-I begins to be able to see the "other" as inside and can at last work more creatively toward a psychological democracy. The poet Josephine Johnson has conveyed this imperatively in the lines

> There shall be no Kingdom and no Commonwealth.
> There shall be no classless state, and no abundant life,
> And there shall be no peace—
> Until each of us, each of us,—squirming here in the too-small desk,
> In the too-hot room,
> —Until each of us shall have said,
> "It is I, Lord, It is I!" [2]

In the myth the bad dreams and the sicknesses are symptoms of a new and different sort of transformation process. Specifically mentioned as having the sickness are Big Snake, Rattlesnake, Tobacco Worm, and Spider Ant— all crawlers on the earth, chthonic spirits in one form or another who have figured prominently in the conflicts of the emergence, who have played both positive and negative roles during the upward journey and more often than not have had to be prevailed upon to remove obstacles. They have been in the position of superior powers. Now matters are reversed. Energy from the lower level must be redeemed and healed by energies from a more spiritual source. The eagle sun power (Dinniki, or Eagle Man) has to provide the substances for removing the sickness.

This coming of eagle healing "from above" symbolically joins bird and serpent, the same two creatures found united in the great Aztec hero-god Quetzlcoatl, the plumed serpent. As serpent is cosmic earth power, so eagle is cosmic sky power. Serpent and eagle must join. In the words of the prophet Isaiah, "They that wait upon the Lord shall mount up with wings as eagles." [3] Bayley points out that "the eagle was identified with Zeus and that the European Spread-Eagle is very similar to the American Indian Thunderbird." [4] He also says that often the eagle may be considered as the "Hawk of Gold," symbol of Egyptian Horus.

Eagle Man, whose story is told in the Navaho Bead Chant, came from a lowly and destitute state of inferiority to be a favorite of the gods. He knows well the difficulties of conscious achievement. As for the other healing elements, they are brought by four Dontsos, Messenger Flies, the traditional bearers of wisdom and counsel from the higher gods. These are similar to the two ravens who perched on the shoulders of Odin and were said to "whisper into his ears every scrap of news which they see or hear tell of." [5]

The episode of the Dontsos is of intriguing importance, so it is well to examine it precisely as it is told.

The Dontsos said that this kind of sickness came from a meadow and pond of blue water whence the Dontsos themselves came. Frog Man and the Wolf Chief sent the White Shell Youth-Who-Stands-in-the-Sunlight with offerings, with the Spirit Wind to guide him and a Rainbow to carry him to the pond of Blue Water covered with moss. The youth blew over the pond at the east four times, and it opened a dark place below and over the east door where there was a black star. There were blue, yellow and white houses there . . . ; each had the appropriately colored star over it, and there were four youths sitting on stools in the houses. . . . They were all very beautiful, and they greeted the messenger.

These four beautiful youths were youths of poison weeds and plants. They became the medicine men who went with White Shell Youth to heal the people—another example of the "psychological homeopathy" discussed earlier.

Who is White Shell Youth-Who-Stands-in-the-Sunlight? Although he does not play a large role in this myth, certain of his possible meanings can be hinted at. White Shell is the "jewel" or stone of the east direction, which in turn is the place of sunrise and renewal. Also, White Shell belongs to one aspect of the great mother-goddess of the Navaho. The young men of the poison weeds, moreover, are below the water and are each related to a star. Also, in their world the east has a black star, indicating that this is a dangerous place. Thus it would appear that White Shell Youth, flying with the aid of Spirit Wind and a Rainbow, surely can be recognized as a prevision of the young sons of the Earth Mother and as akin to such solar or spring rebirth heroes as Horus, Adonis, Dionysus, or Balder who is described as having a power of light beaming from his face.[6]

Curtin says of a major hero figure among many Indian groups: "Under whatever name he appears this benefactor is really that warm light which we see quivering, waving, and dancing above the earth in fine weather."[7] The solar god is the young reborn spirit, related both to the spring shoots of grain, which can be either masculine or feminine, and to the sunlight, most assuredly masculine in meaning. What he is required to do here is essentially what many such heroes have to do: to go to the place of the maternal water, to open the dark womb, and to call out the purposive male aspects which alone seem to have the power to exorcise those poisons springing from their own negative manifestation. If Ackerman[8] and Müller[9] are correct in suggesting that Moon and Star religions are earlier than Sun religions, then this brief episode could be a most vital wresting of Sun consciousness from the Moon and Star realm of the unconscious, a move from Mother to Father awareness.

The twelfth crop is now planted, and the children are growing up. Then an episode occurs quite unlike any preceding one in the myth, as if a fresh dimension were being added:

> Holy Girl often went to the shores of the river, and the people had noticed that she was approaching delivery, though it was known that she had no husband. And indeed she had given birth at the shore to something in the shape of a ball, of black color, but without legs or arms. The next day it had grown bigger, this round thing. Then Holy Girl related a dream. "You only imagine that you have given birth to that thing; in reality you did not," someone said to me . . . who the speaker was I do not know, but he told me to think the matter over. And he continued, "It is the child of the folded dawn. It is the child of the evening twilight folded," he said. "It is a gourd," he told me. The people watched this strange object for twelve days; then it burst open and two boys were inside, and they were born as if from the egg of a bird.

These two boys grow up rapidly, but they will not speak and finally they disappear from sight. Meanwhile Coyote has learned "the secret of the floating water"; he finds a child there, envelopes it in sunlight, and hides it. Then he replaces the light. Floods then begin to rise, and the people for the first time are afraid and call on First Man for aid. They say: "Why should these waters rise and come upon us . . . ? Somebody must have stolen that child, otherwise we should hear its cry. But do we hear it? No. Therefore someone has carried off the child of Water Monster, therefore these waters are upon us." First Man builds four mirage mountains, but even on the top of these the people are not safe from the rising waters.

Then the boys born from the gourd-egg appear, one from east and one from west, bringing reeds which they plant, and inside these reeds the people climb to the hard Sky Roof. Finally Locust discovers the stolen child hidden under Coyote's arm. When they find the child, it is covered with "hard sunlight and palpitating perceptibly." "The child fell from the place where Coyote had hidden him near his heart, and Coyote also exhaled the child's cry that he had swallowed. First Man put an offering into the flood and then placed the child on it, and water ceased to flow upward."

It seems clear that this somewhat complex flood story, even before it is in any full sense understood, has to do with the arising of a completely new possibility for the future. The twin-producing gourd-egg of Holy Girl, and the stranger-child found and stolen by Coyote, although they are different, have this in common: both are symbolic presentations of anticipatory future events.

First of all, the egg birth announced the coming of a different form of substance. This mythic motif is very ancient and world-wide in its distribution. Orphic mystery concepts about it were very detailed.[10] Greek mythology tells of the egg of Night from whence Eros (Love) was born.[11] Brahma is instrumental in hatching the cosmic egg.[12] The Egyptian Ptah himself turned on a potter's wheel the solar and lunar eggs.[13] The myth of a fish which becomes a bird and lays eggs which hatch into man is told by the Northwest Chinook Indians.[14] Island groups of the Pacific have similar tales. The "unknown child" motif also has innumerable and well-known parallels.

To recapitulate, the Navaho myth at this point contains these episodes: a husbandless girl gives birth to a gourd-egg; the egg bursts open and twin boys emerge, mature magically, and disappear; meanwhile Coyote has stolen a baby he found in the water; floods begin to come, and the people are afraid; First Man and the "egg-birth" twins provide mountains and reeds for escape from the rising floods; finally the stolen baby is discovered in Coyote's possession, is returned to the waters, and the floods cease.

The magic egg, the virgin birth, the unknown foundling child, theft, flood—what an impressive array of cosmic archetypes is spread before us! The "child" at this point is not single but multiple, indicating that the individual "self"-consciousness has not yet been fulfilled. Jung has said that the plurality of the "child" image, if found in normal people, "is a case of the representation of an as yet incomplete synthesis of personality." [15] The twins who burst forth, disappear, and reappear, the baby who is stolen and returned, are all harbingers of the final emergence after which a more complete synthesis and conscious unification will occur.

It is probable that Holy Girl, the "virgin" mother of this episode, is the same one who is later known as Changing-Bear-Maiden (or Maiden-Whose-Clothes-Rattle), a ruthless, cruel, vengeful woman who kills eleven of her twelve brothers and is herself killed by the last brother. These later events, combined with the naïve unconsciousness of Holy Girl, give to her a strange and shifting quality. She seems to be, as is Maya, the virgin mother of the diurnal rhythms, of the cycle of time, rather than the primal timelessness of Mother-night-and-nature. She it is who is the bearer of the World Egg which contains the dual aspects of birth and death, east and west, beginning and end. With time she becomes more terrible, more cruel, more inhuman, because in a sense she is herself precisely Time the devourer, the inevitable passage of nature's time which binds man to the wheel of metabolic change and decay. Yet from her come the two boys who bring the saving reeds and who later will carry Sun and Moon. At this point it is as if she were hardly aware of what timeless things had come from her. Consequently her twins soon disappear, and the emphasis shifts to the "foundling" child and to Coyote's theft.

Man does so desire, in his better hours, to outwit the temporal and to transcend nature's rhythmic tides by illuminating both spirit and nature. (This comes later with the carrying of Sun and Moon by the "gourd twins.") But before man can be truly reborn in the fullness of his spirit, before he can emerge into the white world of a new day, he must deal again with his own incomplete and shadowed creatureliness, Coyote. For Coyote has stolen the baby, and disaster threatens. This "foundling" infant, obscure of origin, floats on the whirlpool, wailing, and the apparently guileless Coyote takes it up and cradles it to still its crying.

The abandoned or ill-treated baby motif is an ancient symbol of fresh beginnings not understood by the old order. When the baby is destined to become demigod or culture hero, in order to survive for its heroic task it must be protected and cared for. The infant Moses was found and then hidden in the bulrushes. The infancy of Romulus and Remus was similar. The Navaho hero-twins (whose story follows after the creation myth) had to be hidden from the monsters. The mythic elements of the Christian story contain many such episodes: the child born to a virgin, the birth in a stable, the search by shepherds and magi, the flight into Egypt to save the child. The crying infant in the Navaho story is neither a hero nor any being of major importance. Compared with a myth like the Christian one, this particular "nativity" is vague in outline and lacking in any specific human quality. At the same time, however, it is similar to all the others in its stress on the unforeseen events which follow on every spiritual birth.

One of our omnipresent psychological dangers is that new values and resources, new indications of activity, as soon as they emerge from the unconscious levels of our personality, will be seized upon and either destroyed or misused. For example, when the awkward creaturely emotions too quickly try to force into action a new-found sense of meaning, the result is never happy. The waters begin to rise; the unconscious is enlivened, but it threatens to engulf the slowly emerging order in unconsciousness and confusion. This is always one of the critical times in the human growth process: when new values have been discovered, but a hasty seizing of them seems to be leading toward disaster. Is the only answer to flee the darkness and imminent inundation? This is never the way out.

Part of the answer lies in the unappealing but healing recognition by each of us that our new psychological babies, having floated more or less helplessly within the reach of consciousness, are almost always stolen. That is to say, our very imperfection, so needful of new life, greedily takes over that life and tries to absorb it in the everlasting but futile struggle for perfection. (Often this is indicated quite directly by dreams of babies being found and then lost, or abandoned, or dressed in adult clothes, or kidnaped.)

Coyote, in his ability to find the mysterious wailing baby, shows his quality of relatedness to higher consciousness. His tender treatment of the foundling emphasizes this. Yet he hides the baby, not to protect it from monsters, but evidently only because he wants to have its secret for himself alone. This element of positive/negative—thus, polarized—humanness is omnipresent in the evolution of consciousness, whether at a personal or a cultural level. Coyote, with his virtuosity of manifestation, is the carrier of the temporal paradox of existence. He sins, he errs, he wanders, he scolds; yet withal he knows the mystery. So he can never quite be rendered univocal. On the one hand, in an episode preceding the gourd-egg "birth," Coyote appears as a purely sexual disturber, and the men pursue him and shoot him with arrows, almost as if masculine consciousness felt compelled to put blame for imperfection on its earthly and female side. This is that part of Coyote which, as dog, has long been associated with the feminine

in its death-hell-darkness aspect. Erich Neumann says that
Artemis-Hecate, Greek goddess of crossroads, fate, and
death, had as her principal animal the dog, "the howler of
night, the finder of tracks." [16] So even in his sexual aspect
perhaps Coyote is an awakener, inasmuch as the men do
not succeed in killing him.

On the other hand, with the baby episode, we see
Coyote as the thief in the night, the one who kidnaps and
cradles the infant of the watery womb and who must be
prevailed upon to loose the child and free its spirit to return to whence it came. Here Coyote is close to that
description which Kerenyi has given of certain tricksters:
"a spirit of disorder, . . . an enemy of boundaries, a
mighty life spirit." [17] In his thievery, Coyote is the eternal
disturber; thus the "disorder" of becoming rises and falls
as consciousness itself ebbs and flows. While Coyote holds
the baby near his heart, the turbulent waters continue to
rise. First Man places four mountains on top of each other
so the people can climb above waters and reach the Sky
Roof where they find shelter inside a reed. This race between the engulfing flood and the stalwart peaks is part
of the cosmic battle of the forces of unconscious and conscious realms. Heretofore the work of growth and the
maturation of consciousness have gone on in the vessel of
the unconscious inner world. The time is now at hand for
the reach into a clearer realm of light, where the structure
of responsibility can fill in its rightful proportions.

American Indian myth has many such flood sequences,
some of which also include the saving of the people
through reeds or their equivalents. In Mexico and Peru
there are stories that the first earth was destroyed by a
"water-sun"; or that all was lost in a flood except the
people who entered a log and were saved; or that a great
deluge was followed by a new creation of man.[18] Blind
frogs in a lower world caused the waters to rise, according
to the Mojave-Apache Indians, and one young woman
floated to safety and became a sort of divine Grand-

mother.[19] The Nisqualli Indians say that all the first people except one woman and one dog were destroyed in a flood sent by Changer.[20] In the Navaho creation myth given by Klah two floods are described, one similar to the one being considered here, and one coming later to cleanse the earth and precede a fresh creation.[21]

The task of the ultimate thrust through to the final world is a great one, demanding active cooperation from all. Badger, an animal related to north, to danger, to divination, to strength,[22] "began to dig hard at the Sky Roof but failed, and came back to the people covered with mud." Locust succeeds in making a hole through to the upper world, where Badger could not. (The locust or cicada actually does live, as nymph, under the earth and finally comes out, climbs a tree, and emerges in winged form.) Locust, or Cicada, is felt by the Navaho to be a helpful being of considerable power.

The animal energy alone, no matter how intense, is not adequate to break through to the place of transformation. It can only point the way and commence the task. Essentially we cannot use instincts to transcend instincts, but must turn toward those functions of the psyche which seem, in a manner of speaking, more unfamiliar and alien to our earth-boundness. The locust is primarily air-borne and also—a fact clearly noted by primitive peoples—is a creature able to shed its outer shell from time to time. For these reasons, Locust is the right one to penetrate into the highest place and be the heroic protagonist for the anxious ones waiting to emerge. In his courage and wisdom, his superior strength when matched with White Nostrils and the other challengers, Locust is the representative of the triumphant spiritual father principle. It should not be forgotten that Locust, or at least his locust precursors, played a definite role in the First World, where they seemed to be early carriers of the upward wisdom. Each thing, each part system of the psyche, must eventually come full circle and fulfill its place in the emergence of individuation.

While only Locust can push into the unexplored world, other divine beings marshal their gifts to prevent destruction. The Mountain Sheep People (Hunchbacked gods), divinities who carry fertility in their humps and walk high paths without fear, aid in preparing the way by using magical means to push the waters and the roaring water monsters back. So basic earth power is included after all, but in a more spiritual form than Badger. And finally come the spider helpers, Spider Woman and Spider Ant, to spin the webs of sacred colors "over the sky hole to prevent the water from hitting the people below."

What better image could delineate the benign presence of the mother-goddess at this time of need? Although often the spider is a symbol of the Terrible Mother, it is also true that the feminine as weaver is a maker of profound destinies which, lived courageously, become the tapestry of man's striving. Particularly so is the Spider Woman of the Navahos in this category. She never appears as the destroyer—like Kali, Hecate, Medusa—although sometimes she punishes even the gods if they forget her. Characteristically, as here, she gives aid when it is called for, when she is properly respected. She is the quiet holding on in a time of fear. She is protective feminine objectivity. Spider Woman is the unobtrusive but powerful archetype of fate—not in the sense of determinism, but in the sense of the magical law of one's own "gravity" which, heeded, leads always beyond itself toward wholeness. Bayley relates the ancient sun wheel to the wheel of life and destiny, pointing out that it is held that "the universe is created from and by Brahma as the web from the spider." [23] Brahma is also known as the Spinner of Creation.

The Fon of Dahomey have a divine personage who serves as an envoy of the dual creator. Through this divinity man is not completely bound to determinism. "Man is not a slave. Though his fate binds him strictly to the structure of the world, it is no more than the guiding line of his life." This divine intermediary "is not the power of

evil, he may be the bearer of evil or of good, he may protect man but equally he may make his lot harder." Everyone possesses him as he possesses a destiny, "and he must
propitiate him lest his destiny becomes worse." [24]

"For everything there is an appointed time; and there
is a time for every purpose under the sun." Thus wrote the
author of Ecclesiastes many centuries ago, in words which
convey the full flavor of destiny. If a man truly heeds the
"appointed time," listens for its coming and its ripening
deep in himself, thus he can transform a meaningless fate
into a purposive destiny. This is the spider's web. As the
waters fall back, the web is withdrawn and the Light shines
through, and the legion of great Winds is sent in to dry the
land. Twisted Winds, Smooth Winds, Striped Winds, in a
cosmic array armed with the breath of the gods make the
world ready for life.

We could not leave this flood story without at least a
glance at how its particular flavor compares with the well-
known story of Noah in the Old Testament. Certainly the
two myths deal with emergence and rebirth in very different ways, despite such similarities as the hiding of the
people in reed or ark, the sending out of locust or dove,
the drying out of the earth. As we saw in the Horned Rattlesnake episode, the Old Testament parallels are usually
more focused, coming from a higher degree of consciousness (in the sophisticated sense of "consciousness"). They
are thus more masculine, featuring one God whose command is manifest. In the Genesis story Yahweh sees evil,
is filled with regret and grief over His creation, and Himself sends the flood from above to destroy all things save
only Noah and his tribe. "Then Yahweh remembered
Noah" and caused the waters to subside.

How different is the Navaho flood, precipitated by
mysterious subterranean forces from the mother realm
below the earth and dispersed by offerings *to the lower
sources*. In the Old Testament myth, man is being confronted by an ultimatum from Yahweh the father, one

which requires of him a total giving over to the "laws" of the spirit. He *descends* from the flood of Yahweh to the soft and receptive earth. There is far less clarity of outline in the Navaho myth. The effort toward salvation is unspecific, the final concern being a need to push *upward* to the next world of existence. To this end all things work, to be sure. But neither Spider Woman, for all her assiduous spinning, nor any of the other divine helpers consciously articulate purposes or meanings.

Nowhere in Navaho myth is there the sense of deep relationship between man and the divine conveyed in the statement made to Noah by Yahweh:

> Whenever I bring clouds over the earth, the rainbow will appear in the clouds, and then I will remember my covenant, which obtains between myself and you and every living creature of every sort, and the waters shall never again become a flood to destroy all flesh. When the rainbow appears in the clouds, I will see it, and remember the everlasting covenant between Yahweh and every living creature of every sort that is on the earth.

The one God who desires to remember His covenant, who struggles with and grieves for His creatures, who lays awe-ful commands upon them, is not paralleled in Navaho myth. Yet there is in the Emergence story a quiet tenderness implicit in the work of Spider Woman, First Man, the various animal demigods. It is as if the Navaho myth described the rising of the unconscious which comes when we are still unclear and groping toward a dawning of consciousness out of the night of not-knowing. At such times we are not "sinful," for we cannot yet see who we are. Once we begin to "know," however, to read the signs of our own nature, then we are challenged by the floods from above, the divine longing for an "everlasting covenant."

But now, in the Emergence, Locust has broken through; the great winds have worked at the new world. A magnificent climax has been reached in the music of crea-

tion with full instrumentation for the melody of coming
Man. A song given by Klah to go with the Creation says:

> They came through the sky, I came up with them,
> When my spiritual power was strong, I came up with
> them,
> When it was holy, I came up with them.[25]

Then most fittingly the great sounds diminish. The myth
continues calmly, "The world was smaller than it is now,
and Badger and Squirrel went up and found some of it
hard enough to sustain them; they made footprints near
Navaho mountain." Once more the instinctive earth powers must help, must in their humble way test the basic
realities of the new and make the imprint of creatureliness.
It is ready.

Summary

MAKING THE WORLD BREATHE

*The people built various kinds of houses to live in. One
man went back to a lower world, making it the place of
bad dreams, ghosts, and death. The chiefs decided to plan
for life here, and all those people who had seeds gave them.
First Man then placed his five Jewels, and poles arose for a
final Creation Hogan, as the people wanted the world to
begin. Sun, Moon, Sky, Earth, Dawn, Darkness, Winds,
constellations, seasons—all began to be. Coyote spilt the
bag of stars over the sky, with one fixed star called Coyote
Star. Coyote explained the length of the seasons. First Man
covered and breathed on the creation, "and all the things
that lie on the earth and sky and all the people and all the
things breathed and stood up." Male genitalia remained on
the sky and female genitalia on the earth.*

*First Man wanted someone to carry the Sun and the
Moon, but Coyote had taken the voices from all Created
Things, so nothing could move. Several tried to function,*

but none could. Finally Coyote was asked "to call Sun and Moon to life, and he gave a great shout and all things moved."

Coyote wanted to be a mountain, but people refused and called him Roamer. He objected, so they called him First Scolder. Again he objected, so they called him White-Coyote-Howling-in-the-Dawn.

It is ready, this last level of creation, for man—ready for man to stand up as a truly sentient being and take its responsibility upon himself. The first stirrings of a culture are felt in the initial scene of the two lakes in the east with people building mud huts, or wooden houses, or stone houses, and naming the settlements after the type of dwellings. There is here an almost pastoral sense of community being established on the warm, moist, final earth of emergence. Yet much remains to be done. Containment is no longer in the mother-womb, so a new relation to the feminine must be established if life is to be fruitful. Organic vitality remains quiescent. A final and definitive father thrust of consciousness is still lacking. Death becomes one key to the forward motion of creation, both prior to and following the creation of life in this world.

First of all a missing man is seen down in the lower world, which is then described as the place of the dead, of ghosts. It is also related that the persons who looked down and saw the missing man are the cause of strange dreams, and if evil visions come to people, this person of the lower world is the cause. The mother is not left behind, then, but becomes Mother-Time-and-Death to whose womb man will eventually return and becomes also the container of dreams, the alchemical pot. (The ghost-man actually asks for dishes and pots.)

It is precisely this recognition of mortality, of limitation, that is the necessary ingredient for the completion of things. (This is also emphasized in a later episode where death is needed to make Sun and Moon move.) It places man in time and space and boundary. It makes man aware of his potential heights and depths and the urgency of his fulfillment. Individually and personally this awareness of a time-space reality as well as of a spiritual unlimitedness is the mark of a mature and responsible human being. We must look "down" to the place of strange dreams to complement our upward desire. If we live solely in the worlds of dream, vision, timelessness, or solely in the realm of external facts and their clever manipulation, we are incomplete.

Many concrete examples of this one-sidedness could be given—beginning with the psychotic or the suicide, both completely pulled down toward the womb of death, and proceeding to the person who has no sense of time or the demands of reality, to the person who is painfully bound to the clock, the "ought-command," the anxious future, on to the opposite extremes of compulsive ordering of the outer world and manic leaps into the reaches of space. Somewhere along this rough continuum most of the unconscious egocentric attitudes toward time are to be found. But through a recognition of his mortal domain man learns to discriminate more finely and to recognize the unconscious substratum of his existence as the very core of his divinity and immortality. To see the feminine principle as cave from which one emerges and to which one comes home, as pot which contains dreams and visions, as place of withdrawal and return, is also to see the feminine not as *all* but as *part* of becoming. This lets the masculine be released to function in its own right.

With the realization of the two strata—life and death, conscious and unconscious—as separate but necessary related worlds, the chiefs of the people assemble to plan for life on this earth. For eight days they counsel together, and "all the people who had seeds offered them for the future." Conscious creation is here more imperatively present than ever before. In the dark beginning, the darkness itself seemed discontented and restless, the only creator being a dim sense of the need to move. No goal was known. It was as if an embryo, stirred by forces felt but not in any way comprehended, began the struggles leading to birth. And from that point on, the preforms of life have been working upward. The dim and errant vision of wholeness is, for man, the primal push. He sees he must free himself from the comfortable restraint of the encompassing earth, but only slowly does he recognize that behind the urges, conflicts, errors, evils, is a vast creative force needing him for its manifestation.

The first horizontal mandala of directions has changed and enriched. Sacred stones and colors have added their glow. Battles and conflicts have made turbulent the quiet air, the peaceful earth. With the four lower worlds a new vertical mandala has been accomplished and is now crowned by a fifth White World. This is at the same time the fivefold number of humanness and the quintessence of the journey where life and death become two parts of a great whole. Above all, this White World marks the perception that consciousness is a necessary concomitant to life, that the masculine principle must become a creator planning for the future.

So it is that First Man asks the people, "Do you really want the Sun, Moon, and other creation?" Never before has a decision been thus set before them. What do they really want? This is not to be an unconscious tropistic growth response, but a choice, an examination of values followed by a clear negation or affirmation of those values. And they answer, "Yes!" They also acknowledge their own lacks and ask the Holy Ones, the gods, to be the creators. Then a strange thing happens. The myth carefully states that First Man and his companions are evil and live on the Holy Jewels as food, and First Man says, "I can do many things, my grandchildren." Thus the inescapable imperfection of all of life is once again made clear. Father God, or Grandfather God, is both good and evil, and the sacred meanings may be either used for man or withheld from man (eaten by the gods).

This is to say, unless man consciously chooses to be a part of creation, the divine foundations are held entirely within the nonhuman archetypal realm; and from the point of view of man's ultimate fulfillment, this is evil. When man says "Yes" to creation, however, the suprapersonal energies are made available to him. The tremendous Yeas and Nays of God are echoed in the Yeas and Nays of man. God and man work together as cooperators in creation if any real creation occurs. As archetype God seems to say both a Yea and a Nay to man's urgency toward creation and transformation. In this sense, God is good and evil. Man also speaks both a Yea and a Nay to his own urgency, thus bringing himself into the area of ambivalence and paradox, and also being both good and evil. He possesses the "good" of nature and the "evil" of unconsciousness if he does not choose to act toward a new creation. He possesses the "good" of goal direction and the "evil" of going against nature if he does choose. And God (or the gods), as man sees Him, is both for and against change, both wanting His creatures to stay as they are and wanting them to expand for His sake as well as their own. The transcendent aspects of God, the cosmic and ineffable divine ground within which man and the archetypes have their being, these are neither evil nor good, perhaps, but are.

First Man now sets up jewel wands of the sacred colors at the four corners, and a fifth one in the northeast. He breathes on them, and they become a great hogan which he sprinkles with cornmeal. Despite the greatness of the hogan of Third World, this one is yet more numinous and filled with a stirring sense of the vitality of things to come. After the hogan is cleansed, First Man and First Woman take their holy places south and north of the west pole. All the companions of First Man take their places, including Black God (Fire God or Dark God). Coyote does not come into the hogan. The text of the Haile-Wheelwright version better conveys the cosmic quality than would any paraphrase.

First Man then laid down a Turquoise and on it a White Shell floor covering; on that he placed a small perfect Turquoise for the Sun. Next he placed White Shell for the Moon, then a piece of Jet for the sky and Turquoise for the future Earth. He covered these with an unwounded buckskin; then he blew on it and made it as large as a span. Over the Sun he put Dawn, and over the Moon Twilight as coverings. He put Turquoise over the Sky, and over the Earth Sky Blue, and he blew on these, making them as long as a person's forearm. . . . Then he breathed again and increased the size of the Sun, Moon, Sky and Earth to arm's length; he breathed again and they grew as large as from breast to finger, and the Sun and Moon were elliptical. He then placed the Sun and Moon and Sky and Earth and spread white medicine on them; he also spread on them blue and pink medicine, and wrapped them with rock crystal.

First Man put a streak of Twilight across the Sun's chin and a streak of Dawn across his forehead. He then made balls of the four jewels, and of stone and mica; these became the eyes of the Sun, Moon, Sky and Earth, and their mouths also. He covered their faces with Dawn, which became the awakening of their eyes; then he put Darkness over them and caused them to sleep. He put winter and summer dew into their eyes. . . . He then breathed from the east, south, west and north, and from above downward. He placed White Shell and Jet on the breasts and backs of the Sun, Moon, Sky, and Earth, and these warmed them. He also placed Abalone (Twilight), representing summer, on their breasts, and Sky Blue with Red White Stone on their backs, representing winter. They were to feed on Jewels, and First Man placed the White Wind, Abalone Wind, Turquoise, Jet and Red-White Wind to the right of them, and six winds,—White, Yellow, Blue, Dark, Spotted and Left-handed Winds—on the left. With the first five Winds, he blew upon the Sun, Moon, Sky and Earth from the four directions, and they came to life.[26]

How moving is this Navaho creation, as the creator-god carefully and patiently makes the cosmos from the jewels which are his own food and breathes his life force into what he has so made! Slowly the cosmic elements of Sun and Moon, Sky and Earth, expand as he breathes upon them. He treats them reverently and yet as if they were children newly come. And truly they are, for until now they have been embryos in the womb of the mother.

There is a beautiful parallel episode from the Pawnee where male Morning Star and female Evening Star give to each other all their powers "for the sake of the people." [27] Sun and Moon are placed and functioning. Then "the four World-Quarter Gods struck downward, with closed hands, and on each side of the waters the earth rose up."

When man is confronted consciously by the tidal rhythms of his life, is no longer merely cradled in them as a blind infant creature, it is as though God for the first time laid before man the greater spirit of things, saying: "Here, and here, and here, and here is my world and your world —sky above, earth below, sun as the light of spirit, moon as the light of substance. They are small and large, awe-ful and delightful. They are warm because I warmed them with my Jewels. They rise and fall from summer to winter and back again. They are yours because you chose them, mine because I attended your choice."

Now the jewels for the holy mountains of the future are put in place. And Black God places the various constellations of stars, blows across the Sky to make the Milky Way. "Various people in the Hogan placed seeds of trees, plants and images of animals, which were to be used in dressing the earth." Then "Coyote came in and said 'What is going on?' And snatched the bag of stars and spilled them all over the sky. But he caught one and threw it to the south and it became the Coyote Star (the 'no move' star.)" So the choice of the people, making the creation theirs, is being carried out by the manifold God even into stellar space. Yet the immovable guiding point in the universe comes from the essence of man's creaturely and paradoxical protagonist, Coyote. In effect, this places the final responsibility for orientation in the god-created world directly on the individual man. It is he who must say "Yes!" to the meaningfulness of creation, he who must, in the impulsive and questioning way of Coyote, upset the perfection of divine order and, spilling the bag of stars, find his own axis.

The myth continues with the creation of seasons, mountains, birds, winds, while songs of the Blessing Way are sung by First Man and First Woman.

> Then First Man covered the Creation with Dawn, Twilight, Sky Blue and Dark Sky from the four directions, and breathed four times on it; then he removed the coverings, and everything in the Earth and Sky began to move. Then he covered them again and breathed on them again, and they increased in size; but life had not yet come into them. Four times he repeated this process until they were big enough; then he took up the nine winds from the earth side and breathed with them on the prayer sticks and the mountains, and all the things that lie on the earth and sky and all the people and all the things breathed and stood up.
>
> The genitalia of man remained on the sky and the genitalia of woman remained on the earth, and the nine winds of earth belonged to those who used them as a means of movement.
>
> First Man now called for two youths to carry the Sun and Moon. Coyote had been going about taking the voices from all Created Things, which were now all breathing; but they did not move, and First Man called for someone to help move them. They chose a White Shell youth, but he could not call to the Sun, so they tried another youth, but he was speechless. They tried two more, but finally asked Coyote to call Sun and Moon to life, and he gave a great shout and all things moved.[28]

This motif of the divine outcry is found in other American Indian myths. Curtin tells how a man's guardian spirit comes and says, "Whenever you call my name I will come, I will give my power to assist you." [29] He also relates that in Modoc myth, the daily resurrection of the sun occurs because he is roused by the morning star. "While the sun exists, the morning star must call him." In the Winnebago creation, after man is made by Earthmaker and perfected by a water spirit, he goes toward the creation lodge shouting, to cleanse this world and to make it more alive. [30] Finally "he took four steps forward and emitted a yell and having emitted a yell four times, life-and-light burst right through to, and emerged from, the very center of the creation-lodge." Breath, or wind, has for untold centuries symbolized the spirit of the gods or God. And Coyote, gathering his breath into the "great shout," is truly in this incident the Hound of Heaven.

The articulation and communication of the meanings of the universe belong to man; they are acts of his consciousness, imperfect though it be. How else can the knowledge of the sacred eternality be manifest except through the crying out of man who, like Coyote, carries within him the voices of all created things? The prodigal sweep of life remains forever unfathomed and thus useless unless the individual finds his unique speech to relate it to himself. When the scolding, goading, restless, and disturbing part of man's nature dares—and is permitted—to step forward and shout, all things move, and existence has meaning and worth. To dare this, to permit this, is always difficult because it is difficult to let the last be first, the lesser be greater. A kind of true innocence is required; and for all his brashness and slyness, Coyote preserves a forthright innocence enabling him to trust his immediate responses. And this is, despite man's frequent protests and strivings for perfection, a very basic part of Creation.

It is of value, to be sure, to learn to be objective enough to stand apart and observe the great events within the psyche. But valuable though it may be, and difficult, it is not enough. In fact, it has a dangerous quality in it of luring man into that inaction based on an arrogant worship of the suprapersonal processes. The relationship between human and archetypal meanings is double-edged. If we become enmeshed in the subjective and always immediately personal meanings of event, we never know the awesome and humbling mystery of the movements of the "eternal presences"; we never are filled with the life beyond our own, which carries the balm of sunlight and silent peaks and starlit sky.

On the other hand, to be lost in contemplation of the heavens and so let the dinner burn is the second edge. Its cut is as sharp as the first edge, for it can sever us from the necessary tie to time and circumstance, can make us unrelated and intolerable. When the two youths assumed the weight of Sun and Moon, had the people and gods at that point been content with the beauty and wonder of the fixed creation, no word, no spirit, would have come to set things moving. In the famous Arthurian legends of the Holy Grail and of the various Knights of the Round Table, the fate of the Grail and its ineffable redemptive mystery lay in the hands of Parsifal, the "guileless fool." [31] So with each individual life. Even though a great magnificence of substance is in place and recognized and discriminated, man's roguish human selfness must participate in setting *his* world moving through *his* space and time. This the gods cannot do.

The instant that all things move, "naming" begins. The Navaho believes that when a thing is named, it becomes. This is a rare sensitivity to the essential dignity of all persons and things, and one not particularly evident in our later American culture. For us names are too often classifications, or indications of possession, or ways to impress or belittle. Could we but remember, when a plant or a person reveals to us its name, that it is offering to us a small glimpse of its inward glory, in the same way of revelation as comes to a child when he for the first magic moment sees his loved companion as "dog." The poet Rilke has said:

> . . . Are we, perhaps, here just for saying: House,
> Bridge, Fountain, Gate, Jug, Olive tree, Window,—
> possibly: Pillar, Tower? . . . but for saying, remember,
> oh, for such saying as never the things themselves
> hoped so intensely to be. . . .[32]

So the created seasons, mountains, elements, animals, "told their names." And in this telling, simple and sure, is the essence of the descent of timelessness into time; the personal meaning and function of each aspect of creation is affirmed and accepted.

Coyote, too, wants a name, but for him it is harder to come by. The others seem to have some sense of who and what they are, while Coyote, with his usual restless knowing/unknowing nature, first reached beyond himself for "Mountain," then resisted only a partial identity as "Scolder," and finally agreed to the name "White-Coyote-Howling-in-the-Dawn." He cannot be the holy mountain, for creature being in all its contradictoriness is not and can never be the total height of the spirit. At the same time, he is more than just Roamer, or Scolder. In Winnebago myth, Hare, who also is a trickster and a paradox, is nonetheless a saviour.[33] So, too, is Coyote, in a certain way at least. Clearly this brief but significant scene of Coyote's naming illustrates the ways in which man wrestles with the erring divinity within him—wanting on the one hand to elevate it to the dwelling place of the gods, and on the other hand to castigate it as only a frustrating wanderer, never knowing its own mind, or as an irritation on the face of existence.

"What is man, that Thou are mindful of him?" cried the psalmist. What is this urgent, blundering devotion of consciousness, this poor extension of the Self into human reality, that it is so necessary for the fulfillment of the divine sphere? The anxieties, impatiences, sufferings, awkwardnesses—do they truly belong to the creation? In the throes of them, many a person shouts an agonized "No!"

But in White-Coyote-Howling-in-the-Dawn there is a richer answer for man, saying to him that he is a paradox, a combination of spirit and nature, of future and present. Hearing the eerie cry of coyotes in the predawn hours is like hearing the lonely and the earth-bound calling to be included in the vast truth of the immanent day. Whiteness and dawning are promises of grace, of rebirth, of divinity. The coyote howling is the incompleteness reaching for direction, the darkness quivering on the edge of light. For an eternal moment the radiance glows from the temporal vessel, fades, glows again. This is Coyote repeatedly howling in the dawn; this is every man seeking to be an instrument of wholeness.

VII

End and Beginning

Summary

END AND BEGINNING

*Then First Man placed four supports between the Earth
and Sky in the four directions. Trails were made for the
Sun to travel on. The twins born from the gourd-egg, in
the previous world, were chosen to carry Sun and Moon.
Both Sun Carrier and Moon Carrier said that unless someone
died their daily journeys could not proceed.*

*After Talking God and Calling God (House God)
called from the sacred peaks, First Man lifted "the Sky in
the east with a Jet Wand, in the south with a Turquoise
Wand, in the west with Abalone and in the north with a
White Shell Wand and turned it over upon the earth, so
that it rose on the pillars, east, south, west, north, and center, and both Sky and Earth seemed to be swaying as if on
waves."*

*"Now we have other work to be done," the people said.
"We have seeds to plant." But First Man said, "Wait, do
not hurry." He made the Earth and Sky firmer, breathed
in the breath of the Sun's jewels, and built hogans in all the
various directions. Then First Man said, "Now, go ahead
and do for yourselves." The animals began to plant wild
foods. Birds, animals, reptiles, took their places on the
earth. Salt Woman became angry and withdrew, but the
other Holy Ones took their places.*

After some period of time, a child was heard crying for

four days. The people could not find the child. They were afraid. First Man finally succeeded in finding a mysterious girl baby. "[B]elow her stretched a Dawn Cord from the east and from the south a Sky Blue Cord, from the west a Twilight Cord and from the north a Cord of Turquoise. The child was rocking on Dawn and Turquoise Rainbows, supported by these cords." First Man recognized that Darkness was her mother and Dawn her father, and when he took her in his arms he found a small White Wind in her right ear and a small Dark Wind in her left ear, placed there by her parents. She was Changing Woman.

She grew up in four days, reached maturity and wisdom in twelve days, and the Blessing Rite was given for her. She gave birth to the Twin Hero Gods. She was the maker of Man. From here on, Changing Woman's beneficent creative power superseded that of any of the other Holy Ones, including First Man.

THE Emergence myth proper ends with the numinous rites of the ordering of creation, the injunction of First Man, "Now, go ahead and do for yourselves," and the subsequent taking over by the people of the planting of the earth and the finding of their various roles. Neither the birth of Changing Woman nor the heroic adventures of her twin sons actually belong to the Emergence story. The hero-twin myth has been presented by Oakes and Campbell [1] and will not be dealt with here. Changing Woman, however, cannot be entirely omitted, as her presence brings the emergence full circle to the feminine principle in its spiritual manifestation.

But let us turn back for a moment. In the beginning, in the small and the great darkness, life is not Something; it merely Is. Beginnings are not precision. Beginnings are not confusion. They are the darkness drawn to a minute point of nondarkness, and the silence gathered into a small sound. But in the endings, the light has come into a focus, and the sound of accomplished creation rises in the silence.

Endings, as completions of a cycle rather than as finality, are less shadowy, for consciousness has entered into their shaping. Endings are no more precise than beginnings, for each end has in it the germinating seeds of a new and unfamiliar beginning.

There have been five beginnings and as many endings thus far in the Navaho myth. As has been indicated, these successions of worlds occur in myths of the ancient Norsemen, of African tribes, of the Pueblo Indians, of the Polynesians, and others. As Mercier says of the Fon group in Africa:

> The creation and setting in order of this present world in which men live are not regarded as unique events. There has been a series of worlds and, no doubt, a series of creators. . . .[T]he idea of a succession of worlds and creators should not be lost sight of, even if it does not seem altogether clear.[2]

And how is this cycle of emergence in the Navaho myth, from the lowest level of the dark unshaped First World into this fifth White World, completed? The dramatic climax is found in the placing of the supports between Earth and Sky and the raising of Sky on First Man's sacred wands so that Sky lies above Earth. Both seem to be "swaying as if on waves." A similar picture has been drawn in many other creation myths. Egyptian descriptions sometimes told of the sky's being upheld as a heavenly roof by four great pillars. Or the sky was seen as the woman, Nut, bending over the earth, her arms and legs being supports.[3] Polynesian myth told of the separation of Earth Mother and Sky Father, and the Sky Father was raised up and held, according to Maori and Chatham Island versions,[4] on poles or pillars.

In South American Indian myth there is a World Tree which, like Yggdrasill in Norse myth, supports the world. The Winnebagos relate how Earthmaker quiets the restless spinning world by sending trees, grasses, and "island-

anchorers" to hold it.[5] After God made the world, say the
Abaluyia of Africa, in order to keep heaven from falling
in "he supported it all around by pillars just as the roof
of a round hut is propped up by pillars." Another African
myth describes four iron posts upholding the sky.[6]

These supports are the symbols of a divine preparation
for man. In the Old Testament creation the divine preparation is climaxed on the day when Yahweh looks upon His
universe, finds it good, and rests.[7] Here, too, God has separated earth from sea and sky, day from night, light from
darkness. Thus man's world must be upheld and structured
by some purposive power beyond his own. He must live,
psychologically speaking, eternally in time, always between the great Above and the great Below. Jung,[8] Neumann,[9] and others[10] have spoken at length of the bipolari-
ties in man. These have been called the masculine and
feminine principles, the great Mother and great Father, the
Old Wise Man and Old Wise Woman, Eros and Logos, to
name a few. These pairs are not equivalent, but are related
psychologically.

Probably one of the oldest named and recognized symbolic polarities is Earth and Sky. This is the fertile field and
the fructifying rain and sunlight, the place of personal
home and the place of the impersonal gods, the limited and
the limitless. On the earth one lives, builds, plants, makes
boundaries. The sky is vast and unknowable, holding cosmic forces like burning sun and shattering storm. This is
an ultimate statement of the bipolar nature of the suprapersonal forces, the great separation between spirit and
substance, with the realm of man between. Sky and Earth
are not parted one from the other, but are placed in a
position of constant confrontation, joined, but in the
Navaho myth set apart by the sacred and jeweled pillars.
Precisely this region between swaying Sky and swaying
Earth, between the movements of the spirit and the movements of nature, is where the life of consciousness must be
experienced. It is as if man, in his role of seeker for self-

fulfillment and striver for divine awareness, had to sustain the tension of being pulled upward and downward, had to stand with his feet deep in nature and his eyes turned sunward, and here act out his personal destiny.

Because this ending which is an eternal beginning finds man in a new position of consciousness, it also places on him a greater burden of responsibility for himself and his world. This is suggested first by the fact that the twins born earlier from the strange gourdlike egg now become carriers of Sun and Moon. In the gourd-egg the twins were no more than the vague potential of values to be discriminated. After they are "hatched" and then disappear, they are the still ambivalent life-death polarity which must ultimately be faced. Now, as full-fledged bearers of the differentiated Sun and Moon, they are impressive archetypes of the magic and the divinity which move in the psyche. Such is the repeated cycle, proceeding from unconscious unity to a new something reaching the threshold of consciousness, to a falling asunder or a "twinning" (psychological mitosis), and finally to an emergent differentiation.

Thus when these twins take on the weight of the heavenly bodies there is at once a more defined Yea and Nay, a sharper distinction between the light of spirit and the light of nature.[11] The possibility of choice, present since the primal dark gropings of the First World, is unmistakably articulated not only in the acceptance of the burden but in First Man's command, "Do for yourselves." And so to do is also to die. For as it was at the start of this final world, death is again a key symbol. Then it was death related to the unconscious realm; now it is death related to the mystery of sacrifice. Sun and Moon cannot move unless a man dies each day. It is as if the eternal flow of life could continue only through a recurrent sacrifice of the human. This new sacrifice, like the ancient "mystery deaths," holds the idea of God's need for man.

First Man, though he is "evil" as well as "good," and has been obstructive even as he has been constructive, continues to be the prototype of the creative surge. He is the instrument through whom Talking God and Home God are awakened on their holy mountains. He lifts the Sky and causes the Earth to stretch into fullness. It is as if man cannot really begin his own opus until he sees and experiences the creator-god in all greatness and littleness, until he lets himself be in the hands of the ambivalence of that which is not yet realized and yet is longing for realization. This ambivalence is the grandfather of all tangible things.

Here at this ending, too, before another beginning, the triad is emphasized over and over. There are First Man, Sun, and Moon; First Man, Talking God, and Home God; First Man, Sky, and Earth. If, as Jung has indicated, "one" and the "other" (the "two" or the "twins") are an opposition and a tension, thus pushing toward a flux and an emergent, then "three" solves tension because it leads toward the unity of the fourfold mandala. Thus the triadic number is a fitting synonym for the process of evolution in time, and so a symbol for the self-manifestation of God in action.

The eagerness and impatience of the people at this point are very recognizable and human. We also are thus tempted, having reached a plateau or even a peak of insight, to want to plant our seeds hastily. We do not ask if the ground is ready. The quiet words of First Man—"Wait. Do not hurry"—are for us to remember. We need to cherish and sustain our seeds until the earth under us is firm. Then we can hear First Man say, "Now, go ahead and do for yourselves." With these simple words the triumphant emergence is finished, and a fresh creation commences.

Like all beginnings, this one has a captivating innocence. Squirrel starts by planting trees—the kinds of trees in which his own diminutive creature-self can be most at home. Bear, Gopher, Mouse, reptile, amphibians, fishes, Beaver, Otter, birds, Deer—each one plants those things related to his own habits and habitat. In short, what each does for itself is structure a world within which it may be contained.

What the creator-god does is to provide conditions for growth, and then the various aspects of organic being find their unique needs and values. Seen from a personal and human point of view, this means that the individual is not just a passive recipient of divine fate. Rather, he must learn to allow his manifold sides, his inner creatures of water, earth, air, fire, to find their own home places because they know what they are doing. Perhaps this is the first way in which man can realize that he has need of being more than just an unconscious tool of God.

Many of the major forward growth steps come when an individual permits some newly found part of himself to make a spontaneous and small choice of what it wants. For example, in the dream of a man driven by rational demands of outer accomplishment, a young dog frolicked ahead of him and stretched out in a pool of sunlight. This man's conscious attitude was one of "I must will," "I must choose," "I must get ahead." The unconscious statement, like the myth, was countering with, "The ego-centered I is not everything. Other parts know what is good, too, and you must let them make choices." As he worked at this the man began to have a sense of a much wider world to which he could relate and a much fuller consciousness of the meaning of his own life.

But now the myth relates that Earth, Sky, Stars, Sun, Moon, Months, Waters, Wind, Thunders, Clouds, and organs "for bringing to birth"—all these are planted, too. Why this strange contradiction? Have not all these already been created in earlier moments of cosmic ritual? This seems an anticlimax. It is not. Precisely this act of planting in the creature-earth is the necessary condition for making the world a reality. The previsions of the eternal meanings have been established, honored, and celebrated in high peaks of creation. Foundations of the mystery were laid with each sacred hogan and with each fourfold plan. But the divine jewels and the imposing court of Holy Ones, the antiphony of rising and falling light columns, even the antics of

Coyote—none are sufficient finally to realize the meaning of life for man the individual unit. This can be realized only as the eternal presences are brought to earth, so to speak, are firmly rooted in the transitoriness of a single life span. To become is to become in time and space. Otherwise only the idea of wholeness exists, never the actuality. This "planting" of the ideal in the real is what is implied in the Navaho song, "The world is beautiful and we will put the spirit into it."

So the people plant all moving things for life, for place and time, for nourishment, and each takes its particular dress. The myth continues:

> They now proposed to eat. Salt Man and Woman brought salt and others brought berries, but the Wolf objected to these foods and offended Salt Woman, so she walked off, taking her salt with her. . . .
> The Salt Woman walked off to a place near wheat fields and said to the people who went after her, "If you can lift me, I will return." And they couldn't do this, so she went on to Black Lake and finally came to the Salt Lakes near Zuni; there she stayed because, after trying four times, the people could not lift her. East of the Lake is a male mountain and to the west a female mountain. Offerings are made on top of these to Salt Woman, and the people call to her saying, "My grandmother, pour out water for me," and then drink from a place where sacred waters flow from the east mountain.

The divine mother has here shown another face, even as the divine Demeter turned her splendor on the terrified mortals of Eleusis when they failed to recognize her fiery gift of immortality. The Demetrian wrath became at last the beneficence of the Eleusinian myteries, while Demeter herself eventually was, in essence, the grandmother of Dionysos the Olympian.[12] Here Salt Woman, in her anger, establishes herself as a grandmother-goddess presiding over the east mountain. She is related, as salt, to the alchemical meaning of quicksilver, which is cool and close to moonlight and is also akin to the "secret 'transforming substance' which is at the same time the 'spirit' indwelling in all living creatures." [13]

Salt is known to be an ancient symbol of wisdom. *Sal Sapientiae*, the Salt of Wisdom, is still used in Roman Catholic ritual; and the Sophia of Gnostic tradition was associated with salt.[14] Jesus, discussing the problem of responsibility for building a life, said, "Salt therefore is good, but if even the salt shall have lost its savour, wherewith shall it be seasoned? It is fit neither for the land nor for the dunghill: men cast it out." [15] Salt is thus wisdom—wisdom through suffering—and the seasoning of reality; salt is in the sea. Salt Woman in her withdrawal from the people shows herself to be more remote than the all-encompassing mother-vessel. Yet she is the savor, the "smaller-than-small" which is essential to life, requiring of man that he come to her and call out for the sacred waters.

And now all the people have settled in their media, and a great and beautiful house is made for the Sun with sacred guardians at the east entrance. First Man and his companions the Holy People establish their abode. But a final unifying spiritual principle is yet to come. In the beginning the warm, dark earth (Mother-night-and-nature) held all the creatures in her womb. That state is no more. What shall relate the elements of creation one to another? For when consciousness becomes a goal, unconscious totality must be renounced, lost, and the undifferentiated unity falls apart. This unity must be again bound up and comforted, but in another way and by another sort of feminine principle. There is needed a less time-bound Eros life and relationship begotten by the spirit.

Changing Woman is born at this moment, with Darkness as her mother and Dawn as her father. Initially she calls First Man and First Woman her parents, but the winds tell her this is not true, and even First Man recognizes she is not like other children. Soon she refuses their food and eats only the sacred Pollen. After twelve days[16] she is full grown and very wise, her periods begin, and a Puberty Ceremony is given for her, in which First Man is assisted by Marsh Wren Woman and Bridled Titmouse Woman. First Man offers both White Shell and Turquoise, pressing them to the body of Changing Woman "who thereby was made part of the Sun."

Finally Changing Woman quarrels with First Man, First Woman, and the others from the lowest world, saying, "You are not my mother. Others took care of me. You had nothing to do with me." She separates herself from them, setting up her own dwelling in the west similar to the Sun's house in the east, guarded well, rich with the sacred stones. Her twins are born after she is well established in this place. (According to this version of the myth, she conceives by the Sun Carrier, bearing a *boy* and a *girl* twin. According to other variants—*The Navaho*,[17] Klah,[18] and so on[19]—she bears *twin sons*, conceived of water and/or sunlight, thus mothering the warrior heroes who slay the monsters. One version portrays her as two—Changing Woman and White Shell Woman—each bearing a hero son.)

One of the early accounts of the myth[20] tells that two women, the Turquoise Hermaphrodite and the White Shell Woman, were called on by the original Navaho beings to be light bringers. In *The Rainmakers*[21] Changing Woman is called "young woman who becomes old and goes away and comes back young again." The following story is told: All the people together created Changing Woman as something to be perfect and eternal and to rule over them and help them. They created her, beginning at the toes and working upward. First she was diminutive, but in four days grew to womanhood. "When the Goddess was finished, the people said: 'Everybody has helped to make her except the Earth and the Blue Sky.' 'I will be under her feet and support her,' said the Earth. 'I will feed and take care of her.' 'I will look down on the Earth and make her fertile,'

said the Blue Sky. 'I will send the rain to make things grow.'
So they all had a part in the creation."

Kluckhohn and Leighton have this to say:

> Changing Woman is the favored figure among the Holy
> People. She had much to do with the creation of the
> Earth Surface people and with the meeting at which they
> were taught how to control the wind, lightning, storms,
> and animals, and how to keep all these forces in harmony
> with each other. This meeting was a ceremonial of the
> Holy People and has become Blessing Way, a ritual which
> occupies a key position in the Navaho "religious system."
> Changing Woman, ever young and ever radiant in beauty,
> lives in a marvelous dwelling on western waters.[22]

With the advent of Changing Woman (or White Shell
Woman or Turquoise Woman) the character of the last
world of the myth is altered. Before this, it has dealt with
the slow building of the mysteries leading to consciousness.
From here on, the problem is that of developing conscious
action in a world of substantive time. This goddess, in many
respects the most revered in the Navaho pantheon, has as
her ancestral roots both Darkness and Dawn. Fathered by
Dawn and living near the Sun, she is the idea realized, the
"word made flesh." Mothered by Darkness, with her abode
on the west mountain or on the western waters, and being
woman, she is related always to that inner realm where the
"eternal presences" have their source. She is, as her name
implies, a changing goddess, and thus, for all her sun
quality, a moon goddess as well. Her kinship with such
goddesses as Astarte, Isis, Aphrodite is evident.

Aphrodite, born of the severed phallus of Kronos as it
fell into the sea, is sister to Changing Woman, born of Dawn
and Darkness. Moreover, as Kerenyi has indicated, Aphrodite is derived partially from Oriental goddesses such as
Ishtar and Astarte and is herself most changeable in manifestation, being variously love goddess, "goddess of the
bright sky," spring goddess and giver of oracles, even god-

dess of death.[23] The Winnebago Indians tell of a divine
being, the Grandmother, who produces tobacco blossoms
from one breast, corn plants from the other—and each
plant mysteriously goes through all the changes of its life
cycle.[24] In Peru two goddesses, one of animal and earth
qualities and one of a fire quality, represent respectively the
potato and golden maize.[25] A myth of the Mixtecs of Central America describes a goddess who is part jaguar and
part snake. She is the mother of twin hero sons.[26]

All these goddesses are changing goddesses who include
many aspects, even the monstrous, although the latter are
put into order and form. Changeability becomes the object
of the highest consciousness. The process of the journey in
time is begun when consciousness (the Sun) relates to the
changing unconscious flow (Changing Woman). In Navaho myth, one feels the great goddess to be more than
moon goddess, more than love goddess, more than Earth
Mother. She is the spiritual-psychic aspect of the feminine,
the image contained in the idea, presiding over the making
of man and the war against the monsters. As such, she goes
beyond nature, beyond the lunar cyclic rhythms of primitive existence; this is indicated in Changing Woman's dis-
avowal of First Man and First Woman as parents.

It is of inestimable importance that the individual seeking self-fulfillment be deeply aware of this spiritual feminine principle and distinguish between it and the more
archaic feminine. At the start of life the embryo rests in
the womb of the mother. Likewise at the start of each
psychic pregnancy, the unknown seeds of a later awareness rest in the containing darkness of Mother-night-and-
nature. This is as it should be and must be, for healthy
growth depends on quiet and patient germination; the very
young life needs to be protected and kept safe. This is the
role of the archaic feminine, biologically and psychologically. But this aspect of the feminine principle must never
become the ruler, else growth is arrested or even destroyed.
Perhaps one possible distinction between the truly "prim-

itive" and the truly "civilized"—whether culture or person —is the degree to which desire for containment in the archaic mother-vessel has been renounced.

To stay in the womb, or to want to return to and stay in the womb, is thus a stultifying action leading to ultimate death or disintegration. On the other hand, when issuance from the womb is followed by negation of all Eros and feminine elements, as is often the case psychologically, another sort of death threatens. The former death is from drowning, the latter from thirst. The first kind of disintegration can be seen either in cases of extremely dependent passive people who overtly demand the mother-womb from friends, psychotherapists, and material environment, or in cases where a seeming independence overlaps a desire for unconscious containment. Behavior patterns falling into the former class are infantilism, self-indulgence, conversion hysteria, indecision. In the covert "mother-seeking" groups are, among others, those whose independence is withdrawal-in-order-to-be-sought, or those who retreat from reality into the undifferentiated world of unconscious fantasy. Those who are in danger of perishing from thirst are more likely to be cold, brittle, hostile, rationally refusing emotions, dominating, imaginatively impoverished. In both kinds of psychological death, the "mother-womb" is the clue; whether it be magnet or repellent, it is negative.

Changing Woman, however, is a personification of that benign and mediating feminine side of the godhead to which both men and women must relate if they are to find life. She is the mother in a transforming and releasing fashion. She is the divine and the eternal *within* the substance and the material. It is to her that one may turn for comfort and sustenance, but always to be thrust out again into the flux of things. One sees repeatedly how essential it is that the modern psyche find a living relationship to this aspect of the Great Mother. For contemporary man has been caught between a too rational masculine attitude toward the world and a compensatory and infantile search for "mother" in the small. He succeeds in splitting the atom, while the use of alcohol and drugs rises. His machine, his bridges, dams, cities, his space conquests, are evidences of a superb scientific mastery—at the same time he pollutes his environment, comforts himself with comic books, demands security, and is unable to tolerate any ambiguity or change.

So, from the place of dark sheltering mother Night, the myth has come to the place of the mother of Change, of her who transforms and sends forth, who stands on the side of whatever forward thrust is needed at any moment of time. Because Changing Woman is impregnated by sunlight and water, thus conceiving the hero-twins, she is flanked on either side by the father power. Because it is woman—because it is in truth Salt Woman, Spider Woman, White Shell Woman, Turquoise Woman—the feminine principle in its manifoldness confronts the masculine principle, and the east-west axis of creation becomes the Father-Mother-God. Yet it is ultimately the transforming feminine who is the mediator and unifier, for, as Neumann has pointed out, the goddess always rules over the twins, over the principle of opposites. "This archetypal psychical world which is encompassed in the multiple forms of the Great Goddess is the underlying power that even today . . . determines the psychic history of modern man and modern woman." [27]

It is right, therefore, that the final making of Man (as the inner Anthropos, the Great Man) should, in most versions of the creation myth, come *after* the miraculous birth and growth of Changing Woman. In the present account, Changing Woman makes the people of the Earth from her own skin, assisted by Sun.

> She made our toes and fingernails of abalone shell, our bone of white shell, our flesh of red-white stone, our hair of darkness, our skull of dawn, our brains of white shell, our white of the eye of white shell, our tears of collected [sky] waters, our pupils of shaken-off stone mica and rock crystal, our ear [lobes] of red-white stone, white shell oval

beads make us hear; our nose was made of abalone . . . our teeth were made of white shell, a straight lightning furnished our tongue, a rainbow our arms, plants of all kinds furnished our pubic hair and skin pores.[28]

In the Klah-Wheelwright version, Man is made by all the gods together.

> They made his feet and his toe nails and his ankles of the soil of the Earth, his legs of lightning, his knees of white shell and his body of white corn and yellow corn. . . . His heart was of obsidian, and his breath was the white wind. . . . They took all the flesh of all the different animals to make his body, and also all kinds of flower pollen. They made him of all kinds of water: rains, springs, lakes, rivers and ponds, also of the black cloud and the male rain, and the sky, and the female rain, and they made his arms of the rainbow. His hair was made of darkness, his skull of the sun . . . and the name of this new kind of human being was. . . Created-from-Everything.[29]

The mother of Change presides over the making of Man. Whether, as in the Haile version, she acts specifically, or whether, as in the Klah version, she is just present, it is precisely her "skin," her earth, corn, shells, obsidian, animal flesh, waters, which imbue man with his variety and his own potential for transformation. Her substance goes into him. It is stirred and fructified by the spirit in the lightning, made ripe by the male sun, pushed onward by the spirit in the winds.

The Ashantis of Africa, long before they had any contact with the Bible, "believed that the Creator gave a bit of his spirit to everyone whom he sent to the earth, and that with the gift of that bit of his spirit—the man's soul—was bound up that man's destiny, what he was to become and to do in the world." [30] Also in their myth, man is formed from the blood of the mother and the spirit of the father. Here, as in the Navaho myth, Man is seen as being made of marvelous opposites growing toward fulfillment.

Thus the self is seen in full maturity. The ultimate task of each individual man is to realize vitally what it is to be created from everything, to become Man, to assume responsibility for a life lived. Each must move into the mystery. The mystery of Being—of being just what one truly is—cannot be experienced through theoretical knowledge and the verbal ability to describe processes and levels of behavior. Nor can it be known through the prevalent pattern of protective coloration labeled "adjustment." We can experience the mystery only by experiencing, to its resonant, painful depths, that which seems to be the not-mystery—our own frail, awkward, lonely, noble self in its joyous incompletion. In one variant of the Creation myth,[31] when the people had come into their final world, with humble wisdom they asked, How can we learn to live here? They built the sweat house for purification, and there they sang the Song of the Holy Spirit of Darkness. They sang, "The world is beautiful and we will put the spirit into it." The vessel of each man's wholeness, the containment of the self—this is the sweat house. Man is *in* it; it is *his*, with God's help, through meditation, introversion, creation, and all the ways of inwardness.

This is not sung easily, this Song of the Holy Spirit of Darkness. This "requires us," as the poet Rilke said, requires us as intensely as we require the song. A call must go out, but man must answer in order to help the inner world of the forms and images of Man, the "eternal presences," become manifest. All may be there in us, everything may be ready for our healing, our redemption, our ability to move in our world. But if our initiative is lacking, nothing goes forward. We must take the way of the mystery. We must recognize that we have many aspects—the above, the below, the dark, the light, substance, spirit—which reflect the divine as well as the human. Unless we are connected with them, the cyclic rhythm of our full selfhood cannot be.

Each individual life is its own myth, filled with restlessness, struggle, emergence, danger, paradox, creation. Ancient myths, such as this Navaho Emergence myth, are valid to us insofar as they deal in symbolic language with our personal myth. For most of us, the individual life myth is not consciously serving us until we are willing to read it, until we are forced to embark on the hero journey of redeeming the lost. Whether or not we prefer it to be so, our life is a journey, and we must go forward or backward, up or down.

In this journey, inescapably, are incorporated all the levels and dimensions of the psychic structure: the instincts, basic drives, and urges; the ego level; social relationships; the differentiation of psychological maturity, the orientation toward both past and future, both oneself and others.

And what does this journey, this hero pilgrimage, require of us? The same thing the earth requires of each of her multitudinous forms of life: to fulfill our own destiny as creatures, to be as rich, as total in our unique humanness as a tree in its treeness. Yet one further step is needed from us which the tree does not have to take. For the tree has not lost itself, since from the beginning it has been humbly obedient to its particularity. Not so with us. We have become confused in the cerebral labyrinth of whence and whither. We have sought to be more than human—that is our greatness—but have insisted on our own definitions of how—and this is our littleness.

If we can but learn, as this myth shows, the simple and hard lesson of emergence, of going into the darker places to follow the restless longing upward, of letting no small thing stay forgotten and unhonored, then we shall be whole. Then we shall be related to the unconscious powers within us of life and God. This is redemption.

Synopsis of Emergence Myth

IN the first dark underworld nine people lived: six kinds of ants, three kinds of beetles. At each of the four directions—north, south, east, west—was a round house like an anthill four stories high, with chiefs at each corner of the world. All the people spoke the same language. There were no stones nor any vegetation nor any light.

After a discussion among the chiefs, in the center the people built a house of four chambers, one above the other, and moved from the lowest room up to the next one.

The beings explored the second chamber out to its edge and found it went nowhere. Then one Beetle, called Pot Carrier, found he had forgotten his pots and had to go back to the first chamber to get them. While the second chamber was larger than the first, there were still no stones or vegetation, no days, no light. Then the first beings met two Locust People, and they all went up to the third chamber.

They soon found this was not fit to live in and wondered what to do. Locust tried to advise them as to a course of action. But the people resented one person doing this and felt that all should participate in the decision, so a council of chiefs was called. The chiefs made a choice, and they all moved upward to the fourth chamber.

The Fourth Chamber was larger, still dark, and from

here the Moving Up or Emergence begins. Present were nine beings: two First Men, two First Women, First Made Man, First Made Woman, First Boy, First Girl, Coyote. Also Fire God (Dark God) was present.

First Man's wealth—Whiteshell, Turquoise, Abalone, Jet, and Red-White Stone—he placed at east, south, west, north, and center.

First Man breathed on the sacred jewels which he had placed north, south, east, west, and center, and five cloud columns arose and met overhead, and midday and night began. Coyote visited each column of light and "changed his color to match theirs. In this manner Coyote increased in importance with the nine peoples of this world. His power increased as he absorbed these different colors." Baskets of the holy jewels were at each compass point, with a basket of evil diseases in the center where the Red-White Stone and the many-colored columns were.

First Man and his companions, and Spider Ant, were all evil. The other Ant People were not.

The columns descended into the baskets, with the central black at the bottom. Coyote explained the secrets to Spider Ant. Ant People then asked how they could proceed upward. Acting on First Man's instructions, and led by him and Coyote, all the people grasped the middle column which raised them to the Second (Red) World. All the evils were taken along. And before they left, First Man rolled up the four columns and tucked them into his pocket.

First Man brought the rolled-up columns from the First World. Sphinx Moth Man and Woman lived in this Second (Red) World, and they had light columns similar to First Man's. Nevertheless First Man placed his balls of bright columns at the cardinal points, with the dark ball in the north as a gift to Sphinx Moth Man, who then blew smoke at them, and they expanded and grew.

Sphinx Moth Man asked the people from whence they had come. Ant People told him and asked him what they should do now. He replied, "I am big, but not very wise and know not how to get at things." Four times they asked him. Finally they offered smoke to him. He blew smoke in all the various directions, and they moved upward into the next level of the Second World.

In the second level of the Second World, First Man caused his columns of light to rise overhead as he had before. He placed a perfect White Shell disk in the center to bring about movement there, but nothing moved. He tried Turquoise, Abalone, Jet, but still nothing moved.

Finally First Man placed the Red-White Stone in the center, and the earth shook. He said, "This portends evil. This is not good, children." The earth-shaking increased, and the people were afraid. Finally the Red-White Stone moved up and carried the people to the next level of this world.

The next chamber of Second World was the home of all the Feline People, who were tricksters and at war amongst themselves. The newcomers joined up with the various warring factions. First Man made some of the Felines his house guardians.

The Feline People tried to injure First Man, coming at him from each of the four directions. Each time, however, their arrows were deflected, and First Man killed a few of the enemies and revived them in exchange for sacred songs. They called him Grandfather and Friend. The Insect deputies tried to get their songs back. First Man's armor was invulnerable, and they only succeeded in injuring each other.

First Man rolled up his armor. Coyote and Spider Ant went about and reported back to First Man that there was much suffering and misery, and Pot Carrier Beetle said that he did not want his handiwork destroyed. First Man then blew smoke in all the directions and swallowed it each time, thus removing the "power of evil from the people of the First World, the Insect People."

This power now entered into First Man and the others

of the original nine Holy People. Coyote reported that all seemed well.

First Man, using Zig-Zag Lightning, Straight Lightning, Rainbow, and Sun Ray, tried to bring about an upward movement, but he could not. Finally he made a wand and set it upright. From the bottom upward it was made of Jet, Turquoise, Abalone, White Shell, and Red-White Stone. On each side of it were four footprints. The people stood on these and were carried up to the Third World. "As a matter of course, First Man never neglected to carry all his powers from one world to another."

When the people emerged into the Third World (eighth chamber)—the Yellow World—they found "one single old man and his wife and another old fellow" living there. These were Salt Man and Salt Woman, and Fire God. Also there were all kinds of Snake People, including various colored snakes who were evil.

All the wicked Snake People and the others "looked at, and studied one another while First Scolder (Coyote), unconcerned, roamed about to give the place the lookover. 'What sort of a fellow is that, boys,' they said, 'that goes about here with no respect for anything!'"

First Man then put yellow and red-and-yellow streaks in the east to keep the white column of light from rising. The people, alarmed, asked four times what was wrong. Finally Dontso the Messenger Fly was prevailed upon to tell them. He said that the streaks represented Emergence, pollen and vegetation, and diseases. Owl, Fox, Wolf, and Wildcat addressed the people. Apparently some gift was necessary for First Man before he would remove the obstacles. "They could think of nothing valuable at first." Then Horned Rattlesnake (Big Snake), who "carried a perfect (nonperforated) shell disk and horns on his head," gave to First Man this perfect shell as an offering. The streaks were removed, and the light column arose in the east.

The people accused First Man of being malicious. He

replied, "It is true, my grandchildren. I am filled with evil; yet there is a time to employ it and another to withhold it."

First Man placed the sacred stones in the four directions with the Red-White Stone in the northeast, breathed upon them, and a white hogan arose on five poles. Into this four-storied hogan all the people came. Coyote kept moving about in the northeast sector, asking what was going on and muttering to himself. First Man assigned places to everyone. He made the four Medicine Pouches for the Upward-Reaching (Emergence) ceremony. Songs were sung. First Man distributed to the nine Holy Ones "all his medicine, good and bad."

The people wanted to move upward, so First Man tried to bring light, but Coyote had interfered with it, for he was angry at being called Wanderer or Scolder. Four sacred stones were offered Coyote by various persons, and they called to him as He-who-calls-the-daylight, and other titles. And "Coyote untied the pillars of light at the east, south, west and north, and so the Sahd (world or holy council) functioned again and became holy. First Man then took down the Hogan, rolled it into a small ball, and laid it aside."

First Man put the five Holy Stones in the center, and they carried the people, who were still evil, into the next world.

This was the Blue World, and better than the preceding ones. There were four mountains in the four sacred colors at the four compass points, and there were valleys and hills and contours on the land. All kinds of earth animals were here, and water animals, and birds of all kinds. There was also the Place of the Crossing Waters, where a north-south stream—placid and cool—passed under an east-west stream—rapid, furious, and warm. And the people were surrounded by water, for the streams also flowed from east to south and west to north. The place where the people emerged into this world was called White-Speck-of-

Earth. Animal chiefs had four-storied, four-colored houses at each of the four compass points. These chiefs, two Wolves and two Mountain Lions, at each dawning gave the people instructions as to how they should work and relate. Nadleh, the hermaphrodite, was there, with grindstones, pots, bowls, seeds.

After three years in which the people played, gambled, and labored together, the nine Holy Ones, led by First Man, decided to build another Magic Hogan, a Round Hogan. Into this Hogan came all the people and seated themselves as before. The Holy Ones brought, in miniature form, all the various sacred stones and jewels. Coyote alone seemed to know the purpose of this ritual and ran about telling everyone that male and female genitals were to be made. Then Coyote said, "No one of you seems to be able to guess what these things are. I roam about and have little sense, but I have guessed all of them. You must all pay great attention to this ceremony since it concerns you all. This shall be Birth." And all the people contributed, to give power to the male and female genitalia.

Many babies were born, and for four years the people grew and flourished, with good crops and food stored away.

One day, after the eighth year of living at White-Speck-of-Earth by the place of Crossing Waters, the Wolf Chief of the north arrived home to find his children uncared for, his wife away, his house unattended. When his wife returned, there was a scene, and she refused to do her work. This went on for several days until finally, because the chief was not helping his people, Nadleh the transvestite (hermaphrodite) was called in. He indicated that he had all that was necessary to the men for planting and cooking, and all the men decided to separate themselves from the women and cross over the river.

Four days and nights of consulting among the men followed this decision. During this period they spent the days at the river's edge, the nights at the house of Nadleh.

Spider Woman helped to make the house large enough. The third night the chiefs said: "Let us retire and see how our dreams will be." Each morning the rivers had changed colors. The men brought offerings to the Place of Crossing Waters. Eventually they crossed the river, at the Place of Floating Logs, in five wondrous boats, carrying with them all their belongings and all the male children. They were beset by a storm, but Sphinx Moth (Tobacco Horn Worm) calmed the waters, and they arrived at a place called Gathering Shore.

For four years the men prospered, their crops increased, sacred rites of various kinds were established. Meanwhile, the women were failing. They had been mating with Fox, Weasel, Badger; eventually both they and the men were pulled into autoerotic excesses.

Nine times of planting and nine times of harvest passed. The women became more and more wretched. They mated with animals and engaged in many sexual excesses. Some of the men, too, defiled themselves with animals. One of them was shattered by lightning because of this and had to be revived and restored by a ceremony which included the divine helpers—Dark God, the hero-twins—and Gila Monsters who "find things by feeling."

Finally some of the women in desperation tried to swim the river. A few were drowned. Wolf Chief called to his wife, "Do you really want to cross?" She replied, "I beg of you to bring us back." The women were brought across the river and a series of purification ceremonies held for them. Owl, Squirrel, Toad, and Frog directed the cleansing. Marsh Wren Woman and Snowbird Woman got bowls of jewels and dew from Pot Carrier, helping thus to sweeten and finally purify the women. And the women moved into the houses of the new village.

Despite the reconciliation between the men and women, all did not go well. Some of the people began having bad dreams. Also, First Man punished some of the men who had been practicing witchcraft, adultery, and the like by causing them to itch and swell. Many weeds came up amid the crops. Some people went crazy. Eagle Man provided medicines for healing. Four Dontsos, Messenger Flies, also helped to heal.

Then Coyote appeared, running about and being troublesome. He was pursued, shot at, finally wounded by the hunter's arrows. Now a child was heard crying near Floating-Water place. Attempts to find it proved fruitless. Dreams were reported, telling that Holy Girl had illegitimately borne a shapeless, black, gourdlike egg. After four days, this egg broke open; two boys emerged, grew up, and disappeared.

Coyote found another baby at Floating-Water, wrapped it in sunlight, and carried it away. Floods began, the waters rose, and the people feared. The two boys born of the gourd-egg returned with tall reeds, and the people went into these to escape the rising floods. Finally, with the help of Locust, the people learned that Coyote had stolen the baby and that this caused the flood. Coyote relented, and the "child fell from the place where Coyote had hidden him near his heart, and Coyote also exhaled the child's cry that he had swallowed. First Man put an offering into the flood and then placed the child in it, and water ceased to flow upward."

Badger, Locust, Mountain Sheep People, made a hole for emergence into the next world, but it filled with water and monsters. Spider Woman and Spider Ant made colored webs to hold the waters back. After four days waters and monsters both subsided, Winds helped to dry out the world, and the people climbed up to it.

The people built various kinds of houses to live in. One man went back to a lower world, making it the place of bad dreams, ghosts, and death. The chiefs decided to plan for life here, and all those people who had seeds gave them. First Man then placed his five Jewels, and poles arose for a final Creation Hogan, as the people wanted the world to begin. Sun, Moon, Sky, Earth, Dawn, Darkness, Winds, constellation, seasons—all began to be. Coyote spilt the bag of stars over the sky with one fixed star called Coyote Star. Coyote explained the length of the seasons. First Man covered and breathed on the creation, "and all the things that lie on the earth and sky and all the people and all the things breathed and stood up." Male genitalia remained on the sky and female genitalia on the earth.

First Man wanted someone to carry the Sun and the Moon, but Coyote had taken the voices from all Created Things, so nothing could move. Several tried to function, but none could. Finally Coyote was asked "to call Sun and Moon to life, and he gave a great shout and all things moved."

Coyote wanted to be a mountain, but people refused and called him Roamer. He objected, so they called him First Scolder. Again he objected, so they called him White-Coyote-Howling-in-the-Dawn.

Then First Man placed four supports between the Earth and Sky in the four directions. Trails were made for the Sun to travel on. The twins born from the gourd-egg, in the previous world, were chosen to carry Sun and Moon. Both Sun Carrier and Moon Carrier said that unless someone died their daily journeys could not proceed.

After Talking God and Calling God (House God) called from the sacred peaks, First Man lifted "the Sky in the east with a Jet Wand, in the south with a Turquoise Wand, in the west with Abalone and in the north with a White Shell Wand and turned it over upon the Earth, so that it rose on the pillars, east, south, west, north, and center, and both Sky and Earth seemed to be swaying as if on waves."

"Now we have other work to be done," the people said. "We have seeds to plant." But First Man said, "Wait, do not hurry." He made the Earth and Sky firmer, breathed in the breath of the Sun's jewels, and built hogans in all the various directions. Then First Man said, "Now, go ahead and do for yourselves." The animals began to plant wild foods. Birds, animals, reptiles, took their places on the earth. Salt Woman became angry and withdrew, but the other Holy Ones took their places.

After some period of time, a child was heard crying for four days. The people could not find the child. They were afraid. First Man finally succeeded in finding a mysterious girl baby. "[B]elow her stretched a Dawn Cord from the east and from the south a Sky Blue Cord, from the west a Twilight Cord and from the north a Cord of Turquoise. The child was rocking on Dawn and Turquoise Rainbows, supported by these cords." First Man recognized that Darkness was her mother and Dawn her father, and when he took her in his arms he found a small White Wind in her right ear and a small Dark Wind in her left ear, placed there by her parents. She was Changing Woman.

She grew up in four days, reached maturity and wisdom in twelve days, and the Blessing Rite was given for her. She gave birth to the Twin Hero Gods. She was the maker of Man. From here on, Changing Woman's beneficent creative power superseded that of any of the other Holy Ones, including First Man.

Notes

Foreword

1. Carl G. Jung, "After the Catastrophe," *Spring Magazine* (1946) (Analytical Psychology Club of New York).
2. Clyde Kluckhohn and Dorothea Leighton, *The Navaho*, 4th ed. (Cambridge: Harvard University Press, 1951), pp. 133-136.
3. *Ibid.*, p. 171.
4. *Ibid.*, p. 122.
5. Leland Wyman, "Origin Legend of Navaho Divinatory Rites," *Journal of American Folklore*, XLIX (1936), pp. 134-142.
6. Gladys Reichard, *Navaho Religion*, 1st ed., Bollingen Series XVIII (New York: Pantheon, 1950).
7. Kluckhohn and Leighton, *op. cit.*
8. Father Berard Haile, "Origin Legend of the Navaho Evilway," manuscript, Museum of Navaho Ceremonial Art, Santa Fe, New Mexico.

I. Prologue

1. F. S. C. Northrop, *The Meeting of East and West*, 3rd ed. (New York: Macmillan, 1946).
2. Albert Schweitzer, *Indian Thought and Its Development*, 1st ed. (New York: Holt, 1936).

II. Forms and Images

1. W. Max Müller, in L. H. Gray, ed., *Mythology of All Races*, 1st ed. (Boston: Marshall Jones, 1918), XII, pp. 68 ff.
2. S. Langdon, *The Babylonian Epic of Creation*, 1st ed. (Oxford: Clarendon Press, 1923), pp. 67 ff.
3. Harold Bayley, *The Lost Language of Symbolism*, 4th ed. (London: Williams and Norgate, 1952), II, 14.

4. Mary Briner, unpublished thesis, C. G. Jung Institute, Zurich, Switzerland, 1955.

5. Matilda Coxe Stevenson, *The Zuni Indians* (Washington: 23rd Annual Report of the Burial of American Ethnology, 1901–1902), p. 23.

6. Lewis Spence, *Myths and Legends of Mexico and Peru,* Panoramic ed. (Boston: David D. Dickerson) p. 118.

7. *Popol Vuh*, translated by Delia Goetz and S. G. Morley (Norman: University of Oklahoma Press, 1950).

8. *Ibid.*, p. 81.

9. Brian Branston, *Gods of the North*, 1st ed. (London: Thames and Hudson, 1955), p. 52.

10. *The Bible*, American Translation (Chicago: University of Chicago Press, 1935), Genesis 1:1–5.

11. Natalie Curtis, ed., *The Indians' Book*, 1st ed. (New York: Harper, 1907), p. 315.

12. J. Curtin, *Creation Myths of Primitive America*, 1st ed. (London: Williams and Norgate, 1899), p. xiii.

13. Marcel Griale *et al.*, *African Worlds*, 2nd ed. (London: Oxford University Press, 1955), pp. 84 ff.

14. Washington Matthews, "Navajo Legends," *Memoirs of the American Folklore Society*, V (1897), 63–64.

15. Stevenson, *op. cit.*, pp. 87–88.

16. Sir Baldwin Spencer and F. J. Gillen, *The Arunta*, 1st ed. (London: Macmillan, 1927), I, 306–307.

17. Bayley, *op. cit.*, I, 208.

18. Spence, *op. cit.*, p. 25.

19. *Ibid.*, p. 305.

20. A. L. Kroeber, "Wishosk Myths," *Journal of American Folklore*, XVIII (April–June, 1905), 89–94.

21. Paul Radin, *The Origin Myth of the Medicine Rite: Three Versions*, Special Publication of Bollingen Foundation, No. 2 (Baltimore: Waverly, 1950), p. 38.

22. Ella E. Clark, *Indian Legends of the Pacific Northwest*, 2nd ed. (Berkeley: University of California Press, 1953), p. 133.

23. Frank Cushing, *Zuni Breadstuff*, Indian Notes and Monographs VIII, Museum of American Indians (New York: Heye Foundation, 1920), pp. 19–21.

24. Maurice Maeterlinck, *The Life of the Bee* (New York: Dodd, Mead, 1901), p. 35.

25. Mary R. Coolidge, *The Rain-Makers*, 1st ed. (New York: Houghton Mifflin, 1929), pp. 179–181.

26. Branston, *op. cit.*, p. 47.

27. Radin, *op. cit.*, p. 9.

28. Curtis, *op. cit.*, p. 96.

29. Paul Radin, "Religion of the North American Indians," *Journal of American Folklore*, XXVII (October–December, 1914), 360 ff.

30. Griale *et al.*, *op. cit.*, pp. 155, 191–193.

31. *Ibid.*, pp. 85 ff.

32. Cushing, *op. cit.*, p. 19.

33. Father Berard Haile, *Head and Face Marks in Navaho Ceremonialism* (St. Michaels, Ariz.: St. Michaels Press, 1947), pp. 3 ff.

34. Franc Newcomb *et al.*, *A Study of Navajo Symbolism*, Papers of the Peabody Museum of Archaeology and Ethnology, Harvard University, XXXII, No. 3 (1956), 12.

35. Branston, *op. cit.*, p. 152.

36. C. Kerenyi, *The Gods of the Greeks*, 1st ed. (London: Thames and Hudson, 1951), pp. 15–19.

37. Bayley, *op. cit.*, I, 196–198.

38. A. H. Gayton and Stanley Newman, "Yokuto and Western Mono Myths," *Anthropological Record*, V, No. 1 (University of California Press, 1940), p. 19.

39. *Ibid.*, p. 41.

40. *Ibid.*

41. T. R. Henn, *The Harvest of Tragedy*, 1st ed. (London: Methuen, 1956), p. 21.

42. Maud Oakes, unpublished version of Navaho Feather Chant, recorded in 1942, in possession of Dr. Moon.

43. Langdon, *op. cit.*, pp. 141–149.

44. Bayley, *op. cit.*, I, 75.

45. Gladys Reichard, *Navaho Religion*, 1st ed. Bollingen Series XVIII (New York: Pantheon, 1950), I, 244.

46. C. G. Jung, *Psychology and Alchemy*, 2nd ed., Bollingen Series XX (New York: Pantheon, 1953), p. 193.

47. Ruth Kraus, *A Hole Is to Dig*, 1st ed. (New York: Harper, 1952), p. 7.

48. Father Berard Haile, "Creation and Emergence Myth of the Navaho" (original text, at Museum of Navaho Ceremonial Art, Santa Fe, N.Mex.), p. 349.

49. Hartley B. Alexander *et al.*, in Gray, *op. cit.*, X, North American, xxiii.

50. Jung, *op. cit.*, p. 154.

51. Clyde Kluckhohn and Dorothea Leighton, *The Navaho*, 4th ed. (Cambridge: Harvard University Press, 1951), p. 124.

52. Langdon, *op. cit.*, pp. 67–71.

53. Gray *op. cit.*, VI, 275 ff.

54. *Ibid.*, XII, 68–73.

55. Stevenson, *op. cit.*, pp. 22–23.

56. Griale *et al.*, *op. cit.*, pp. 217–219.

57. Spencer and Gillen, *op. cit.*, I, 359.

58. Curtis, *op. cit.*, p. 97.

59. *Popol Vuh*, pp. 78–80.

60. *Ibid.*, p. 81.

61. *Ibid.*, p. 82.

62. Mary C. Wheelwright, *Navajo Creation Myth* (Santa Fe: Museum of Navaho Ceremonial Art, 1942), pp. 40–41.

63. Bayley, *op. cit.*, I, 310.

64. Curtin, *op. cit.*, p. 506.

65. Clark, *op. cit.*, p. 193.

66. *Ibid.*, p. 172.

67. C. H. Merriam, *The Dawn of the World*, 1st ed. (Cleveland: Arthur H. Clark, 1910), p. 20.

68. Gayton and Newman, *op. cit.*, pp. 31–32.

69. Bayley, *op. cit.*, II, 102–109.

70. Radin, *Origin Myth*, pp. 10, 40–41.

71. Paul Radin, *The Trickster*, 1st ed. (London: Routledge and Kegan Paul, 1956), p. x.

72. Paul Radin, *Winnebago Hero Cycles* (Baltimore: Waverley, 1948), p. 18.

73. Radin, *The Trickster*, p. x.

74. Spencer and Gillen, *op. cit.*, I, 306.

75. Ruth Bunzel, *Introduction to Zuni Ceremonialism* (Washington: 47th Annual Report of the Bureau of American Ethnology, 1932), p. 481.

76. Father Berard Haile, in *Head and Face Masks*, points out that the "nine group" is usually associated with witchcraft. The problem of witchcraft and evil is discussed in later sections of this volume.

77. Color-direction sequences in Navaho myths and chants have been elaborately studied and recorded, and the major studies are referred to in this volume. No attempt will be made here to enter into a discussion of the complexities and contradictions involved in color-direction symbolism. All statements in this volume are based on the sequences found in the particular myth being considered, and all interpretations are the responsibility of the author.

78. Bayley, *op. cit.*, I, 211 ff.

79. *Ibid.,* II, 96.
80. Newcomb, *op. cit.,* p. 15.
81. Griale *et al., op. cit.,* pp. 219–221.
82. Bayley, *op. cit.,* I, 210.
83. Jung, *op. cit.*
84. *Ibid.,* p. 162.
85. Stevenson, *op. cit.,* p. 23.
86. Griale *et al., op. cit.,* p. 221.
87. Langdon, *op. cit.,* pp. 57–59, 215–217.
88. Matthew W. Stirling, "Origin Myth of Acoma and Other Records," *Bureau of American Ethnology Bulletin,* CXXXV (Washington: Government Printing Office, 1942), 33.
89. M. K. Munitz, ed., *Theories of the Universe* (Glencoe: The Free Press, 1957), pp. 67 ff.
90. Katharine Spencer, *Reflection of Social Life in the Navaho Origin Myth,* University of New Mexico Publications in Anthropology, No. 3 (1947), pp. 106–108.
91. L. C. Wyman and Clyde Kluckhohn, *Navaho Classification of Their Song Ceremonials,* Memoirs of the American Anthropological Association, No. 50 (1938).
92. Radin, *Origin Myth,* p. 9.
93. Griale *et al., op. cit.,* p. 39.
94. Gladys Reichard, "Individualism and Mythological Style," *Journal of American Folklore,* LVII, No. 223 (January–March, 1944), 20–22.
95. Stevenson, *op. cit.,* pp. 29–30.
96. Griale *et al., op. cit.,* pp. 160–161.
97. *Ibid.,* p. 172.
98. *Beautyway: A Navaho Ceremonial Myth,* recorded and translated by Father Berard Haile, with a variant myth recorded by Maud Oakes and sandpaintings recorded by Laura A. Armer, Franc J. Newcomb, and Maud Oakes, 1st ed., Bollingen Series LIII (New York: Pantheon, 1957), p. 166.
99. Newcomb, *op. cit.,* pp. 16 ff.
100. Griale *et al., op. cit.,* p. 187.

III. Conflict of Forces

1. Ruth Bunzel, *Introduction to Zuni Ceremonialism* (Washington: 47th Annual Report of the Bureau of American Ethnology, 1932), p. 25.
2. *Ibid.,* p. 487.
3. J. Curtin, *Creation Myths of Primitive America,* 1st ed. (London: Williams and Norgate, 1899), p. 4.

4. Marcel Griale et al., *African Worlds*, 2nd ed. (London: Oxford University Press, 1955), p. 166.

5. Brian Branston, *Gods of the North*, 1st ed. (London: Thames and Hudson, 1955), p. 73.

6. *The I Ching or Book of Changes*, 1st ed., Bollingen Series XIX (New York: Pantheon, 1950).

7. *Popol Vuh*, translated by Delia Goetz and S. G. Morley (Norman: University of Oklahoma Press, 1950), pp. 86–91.

8. Branston, *op. cit.*, pp. 59–60.

9. L. A. White, *The Acoma Indians* (Washington: 47th Annual Report of the Bureau of American Ethnology, 1932), p. 142.

10. G. R. S. Mead, *Pistis Sophia* (London: John M. Watkins, 1947), pp. 35 ff.

11. *The Bible*, American Translation (Chicago: University of Chicago Press, 1935), Jonah 4:1–4.

12. Bunzel, *op. cit.*, p. 80.

13. Linda Fierz-David, *The Dream of Poliphilo*, 1st ed., Bollingen Series XXV (New York: Pantheon, 1950), p. 34.

14. Maud Oakes, unpublished version of Navaho Feather Chant, recorded in 1942, in possession of Dr. Moon.

15. Gladys Reichard, *Navaho Religion*, 1st ed., Bollingen Series XVIII (New York: Vol. I, Pantheon, 1950), p. 197.

16. Franc Newcomb et al., *A Study of Navajo Symbolism*, Papers of Peabody Museum of Archaeology and Ethnology, Harvard University, XXXII, No. 3 (1956), 16–17.

17. W. Max Müller, in L. H. Gray, ed., *Mythology of All Races*, 1st ed. (Boston: Marshall Jones, 1918), XII, 86 ff.

18. S. H. Langdon, in Gray, *op. cit.*, V, 277 ff.

19. C. G. Jung, *Psychology and Alchemy*, 2nd ed., Bollingen Series XX (New York: Pantheon, 1953), p. 172.

20. Newcomb et al., *op. cit.*, p. 31.

21. *Popol Vuh*, pp. 93–106.

22. Harold Osborne, *Indians of the Andes* (London: Routledge and Kegan Paul, 1952), p. 44.

23. Lewis Spence, *Myths of Mexico and Peru* (Boston: David D. Nickerson), p. 19.

24. C. Kerenyi, *The Gods of the Greeks*, 1st ed. (London: Thames and Hudson, 1951), pp. 20–30.

25. Clyde Kluckhohn and Dorothea Leighton, *The Navaho*, 4th ed. (Cambridge: Harvard University Press, 1951), p. 129.

26. Sara Teasdale, *Dark of the Moon*, 6th ed. (New York: Macmillan, 1929), p. 19.

27. Donald A. Mackenzie, *Myths of Babylonia and Assyria* (London: Gresham, n.d.), p. 195.

28. *Dictionary of Non-Classical Mythology*, Everyman's Library (London: J. M. Dent, 1952), p. 121.

29. *The Bible*, Luke 15:32.

IV. Witchcraft and Holiness

1. Gladys Reichard, *Navaho Religion*, 1st ed., Bollingen Series XVIII (New York: Pantheon, 1950), I, 14.

2. Franc Newcomb *et al.*, *A Study of Navajo Symbolism*, Papers of Peabody Museum of Archaeology and Ethnology, Harvard University, XXXII, No. 3 (1956), 15.

3. Reichard, *op. cit.*, I, 193.

4. Erich Neumann, *The Great Mother*, 1st ed., Bollingen Series XLVII (New York: Pantheon, 1955).

5. Paul Radin, "Religion of the North American Indians," *Journal of American Folklore*, XXVII (October–December, 1914), 356.

6. Marius Barbeau, *The Old World Dragon in America* (Chicago: University of Chicago Press, 1952), p. 115.

7. Melville Jacobs, *Coos Myth Texts*, University of Washington Publications in Anthropology, VIII, No. 2 (Seattle: April, 1940), p. 252.

8. Matilda Coxe Stevenson, *The Zuni Indians* (Washington: 23rd Annual Report of the Bureau of American Ethnology, 1901–1902), pp. 94–96.

9. See Reichard, *op. cit.*, Vols. I and II; Margaret Schevill, *The Pollen Path*, 1st ed. (Stanford: Stanford University Press, 1956), pp. 110 ff.; Father Berard Haile *et al.*, *Beautyway*, Bollingen Series LIII (New York: Pantheon, 1957).

10. Father Berard Haile, *Head and Face Masks in Navaho Ceremonialism* (St. Michaels, Ariz.: St. Michaels Press, 1947), pp. 2 ff.

11. Harold Bayley, *The Lost Language of Symbolism*, 4th ed. (London: Williams and Norgate, 1952), I, 289.

12. *Ibid.*, I, 211.

13. Sir Arthur Avalon, *The Serpent Power*, 2nd rev. ed. (Madras: Ganesh, 1924), p. 3.

14. *Ibid.*, p. 35.

15. *The Bible*, American Translation (Chicago: University of Chicago Press, 1935), Numbers 21: 6–9.

16. Bayley, *op. cit.*, I, 88 ff., takes a somewhat different position, holding that the serpent represents both spiritual rebirth and the

"earth-creeping attitude of materialism. . . . Thus the same object served sometimes as the symbol of two diametrically opposed ideas, and in allegory one meets as constantly with the Evil as with the Good Serpent. . . . During the wanderings of the Israelites the dual symbolism of the Serpent is brought into juxtaposition in the story that the children of Israel were mortally bitten by serpents, and that only those who looked upon the Serpent uplifted by Moses were healed."

17. D. Phillips *et al.*, eds., *The Choice Is Always Ours* (New York: Harper, 1960), p. 93.

18. J. Curtin, *Creation Myths of Primitive America*, 1st ed. (London: Williams and Norgate, 1899), p. 15.

19. S. Kierkegaard, *Christian Discourses* (London: Oxford University Press, 1939), pp. 40 ff., 63 ff.

v. Man and Woman

1. C. Kerenyi, *The Gods of the Greeks*, 1st ed. (London: Thames and Hudson, 1951), p. 15.

2. Brian Branston, *Gods of the North*, 1st ed. (London: Thames and Hudson, 1955), pp. 52–53.

3. *The I Ching or Book of Changes*, 1st ed., Bollingen Series XIX (New York: Pantheon, 1950), I, xxxi.

4. Harold Bayley, *The Lost Language of Symbolism*, 4th ed. (London: Williams and Norgate, 1952), II, 192.

5. A. L. Kroeber, "Wishosk Myths," *Journal of American Folklore*, XVIII (April–June, 1905), 91.

6. Linda Fierz, unpublished notes from seminar given in 1948, C. G. Jung Institute, Zurich, Switzerland.

7. Marcel Griale *et al.*, *African Worlds*, 2nd ed. (London: Oxford University Press, 1955), p. 219.

8. Margaret Schevill, *The Pollen Path*, 1st ed. (Stanford: Stanford University Press, 1956), p. 76.

9. *The Bible*, American Translation (Chicago: University of Chicago Press, 1935), Mark 8:36.

10. *Ibid.*, Luke 9:62.

11. Culver Barker, unpublished seminar given at C. G. Jung Institute, Zurich, Switzerland, 1955.

12. Erich Neumann, *The Great Mother*, 1st ed., Bollingen Series XLVII (New York: Pantheon, 1955), p. 33.

13. J. Curtin, *Creation Myths of Primitive America*, 1st ed. (London: Williams and Norgate, 1899), pp. 121 ff.

14. Branston, *op. cit.*, p. 121.

15. Bayley, *op. cit.*, I, 85–88.

16. *I Ching*, vol. I, p. 47.

17. Linda Fierz-David, *The Dream of Poliphilo*, 1st ed., Bollingen Series XXV (New York: Pantheon, 1950), p. 39.

18. C. G. Jung *et al.*, *The Mysteries*, 1st ed., Bollingen Series XXX–2 (New York: Pantheon, 1955), p. 93.

19. Griale *et al.*, *op. cit.*, p. 150.

20. Jung *et al.*, *op. cit.*, p. 115.

vi. Consummation

1. Father Berard Haile and Mary Wheelwright, *Emergence Myth*, 1st ed. (Santa Fe: Museum of Navaho Ceremonial Art, 1949), pp. 16 ff.

2. Josephine Johnson, *Year's End*, 1st ed. (New York: Simon and Schuster, 1937), p. 77.

3. *The Bible*, American Translation (Chicago: University of Chicago Press, 1935), Isaiah 40:31.

4. Harold Bayley, *The Lost Language of Symoblism*, 4th ed. (London: Williams and Norgate, 1952), I, 76, 114.

5. Brian Branston, *Gods of the North*, 1st ed. (London: Thames and Hudson, 1955), p. 117.

6. *Ibid.*, p. 123.

7. J. Curtin, *Creation Myths of Primitive America*, 1st ed. (London: Williams and Norgate, 1899), p. xix.

8. *Hail Chant and Water Chant*, recorded by Mary C. Wheelwright, Navajo Religion Series II (Santa Fe: Museum of Navajo Ceremonial Art, 1946), pp. iii–149.

9. W. Max Müller, in L. H. Gray, ed., *Mythology of All Races*, 1st ed. (Boston: Marshall Jones, 1918), XII, 54–55.

10. C. G. Jung *et al.*, *The Mysteries*, 1st ed., Bollingen Series XXX–2 (New York: Pantheon, 1955), pp. 209 ff.

11. C. Kerenyi, *The Gods of the Greeks*, 1st ed. (London: Thames and Hudson, 1951), p. 16.

12. Heinrich Zimmer, *Myths and Symbols in Indian Art and Civilization*, 2nd ed., Bollingen Series VI (New York: Pantheon, 1947), p. 116.

13. Gray, *op. cit.*, XII, 145.

14. Ella E. Clark, *Indian Legends of the Pacific Northwest*, 2nd ed. (Berkeley: University of California Press, 1953), p. 135.

15. C. G. Jung and C. Kerenyi, *Essays on a Science of Mythology*, 1st ed., Bollingen Series XXII (New York: Pantheon, 1949), p. 116.

16. Erich Neumann, *The Great Mother*, 1st ed., Bollingen Series XLVII (New York: Pantheon, 1955), p. 170.

17. Paul Radin *et al.*, *The Trickster*, 1st ed. (London: Routledge and Kegan Paul, 1956), p. 189.

18. Lewis Spence, *Myths and Legends of the North American Indians*, Panoramic Ed. (Boston: David D. Nickerson), pp. 119, 122, 257.

19. Natalie Curtis, ed., *The Indians' Book*, 1st ed. (New York: Harper, 1907), p. 330.

20. Clark, *op. cit.*, p. 136.

21. Mary C. Wheelwright, *Navajo Creation Myth* (Santa Fe: Museum of Navajo Ceremonial Art, 1942), pp. 48 ff., 100.

22. For animal meanings, see Gladys Reichard, *Navaho Religion*, 1st ed., Bollingen Series XVIII (New York: Pantheon, 1950); and Franc Newcomb *et al.*, *A Study of Navajo Symbolism*, Papers of the Peabody Museum of Archaeology and Ethnology, Harvard University, XXXII, No. 3 (1956).

23. Bayley, *op. cit.*, I, 138.

24. Marcel Griale *et al.*, *African Worlds*, 2nd ed. (London: Oxford University Press, 1955), pp. 228–229.

25. Klah, *op. cit.*, p. 132.

26. Haile and Wheelwright, *op. cit.*, pp. 42–43.

27. Curtis, *op. cit.*, p. 103.

28. Haile and Wheelwright, *op. cit.*, p. 45.

29. Curtin, *op. cit.*, p. xxviii.

30. Paul Radin, *The Origin Myth of the Medicine Rite: Three Versions*, Special Publication of Bollingen Foundation, No. 2 (Baltimore: Waverly, 1950), p. 57.

31. Ernest Newman, *The Wagner Operas*, 1st ed. (New York: Knopf, 1949), p. 643. See also H. A. Guerber, *Myths and Legends of the Middle Ages* (London: Geo. G. Harrap, 1909), pp. 250–267.

32. Rainer Maria Rilke, *Duino Elegies* (New York: Norton, 1939), p. 75.

33. Paul Radin, *The Road of Life and Death*, 1st ed., Bollingen Series V (New York: Pantheon, 1945), pp. 21–33 and throughout.

VII. End and Beginning

1. See Maud Oakes and Joseph Campbell, *Where the Two Came to Their Father*, 1st ed., Bollingen Series I (New York: Pantheon, 1943).

2. Marcel Griale *et al.*, *African Worlds*, 2nd ed. (London: Oxford University Press, 1955), pp. 217 ff.

3. W. Max Müller, in L. H. Gray, ed., *Mythology of All Races*, 1st ed. (Boston: Marshall Jones, 1918), XII, 35 ff.

4. Roland B. Dixon, in *ibid.*, IX, 31 ff.

5. Paul Radin, *The Road of Life and Death*, 1st ed., Bollingen Series V (New York: Pantheon, 1945), pp. 17–18.

6. Griale *et al.*, *op. cit.*, pp. 28, 221.

7. *The Bible*, American Translation (Chicago: University of Chicago Press, 1935), Genesis 1:31.

8. C. G. Jung, *Integration of the Personality* (New York: Farrar and Rinehart, 1939).

9. Erich Neumann, *The Great Mother*, 1st ed., Bollingen Series XLVII (New York: Pantheon, 1955).

10. See such divergent writers and books as H. G. Baynes, *Mythology of the Soul* (London: Methuen, 1949); Eric Fromm, *The Art of Loving*, 1st ed. (New York: Harper, 1956); and F. S. C. Northrop, *The Meeting of East and West*, 3rd ed. (New York: Macmillan, 1946).

11. Even so, the Navaho myth never relinquishes the paradox, for Moon Carrier is addressed as "Carrier of the Day, whose Light lies on the ground."

12. C. Kerenyi, *The Gods of the Greeks*, 1st ed. (London: Thames and Hudson, 1951), pp. 252–253.

13. C. G. Jung, *Psychology and Alchemy*, 2nd ed., Bollingen Series XX (New York: Pantheon, 1953), p. 26.

14. Harold Bayley, *The Lost Language of Symbolism*, 4th ed. (London: Williams and Norgate, 1952), I, 228.

15. *The Bible*, Luke 14:34–35.

16. Twelve is a number of fullness or completion in Navaho myth as well as in other traditions. Changing Woman's twin-hero sons grow up in twelve days and start their journey. This has a remarkable resemblance to the so-called "twelve-year-old episode" in the life of Jesus as told in Luke 2:41–50. Twelve months, twelve zodiacal signs—these are only a few of the many "twelves" which need not be multiplied here.

17. Clyde Kluckhohn and Dorothea Leighton, *The Navaho*, 4th ed. (Cambridge: Harvard University Press, 1951), p. 123.

18. Hasteen Klah, *Navajo Creation Myth* (Santa Fe: Museum of Navajo Ceremonial Art, 1942), p. 78.

19. See Washington Matthews, "Navajo Legends," *Memoirs of the American Folklore Society*, V (1897); Oakes and Campbell, *op. cit.*; and Gladys Reichard, *Navaho Religion*, 1st ed., Bollingen Series XVIII (New York: Pantheon, 1950).

20. James Stevenson, *Ceremonial of Hasjelti Dailjis and Mythical Sand Painting of the Navaho Indians* (Washington: 8th Annual

Report of the Bureau of American Ethnology, 1886–1887), p. 275.

21. Mary R. Coolidge, *The Rain-Makers*, 1st ed. (New York: Houghton Mifflin, 1929), pp. 183–185.

22. Kluckhohn and Leighton, *op. cit.*, p. 123.

23. Kerenyi, *op. cit.*, pp. 57–81.

24. Paul Radin, *The Origin Myth of the Medicine Rite: Three Versions*, Special Publication of Bollingen Foundation, No. 2 (Baltimore: Waverly Press, Inc., 1950), p. 48.

25. Bayley, *op. cit.*, II, p. 92.

26. Lewis Spence, *Myths and Legends of Mexico and Peru* (Boston: David D. Nickerson & Co.), p. 120.

27. Neumann, *op. cit.*, p. 275.

28. Father Berard Haile, "*Creation and Emergence Myth of the Navaho*" (original text, at Museum of Navajo Ceremonial Art, Santa Fe, New Mexico), p. 266.

29. Klah, *op. cit.*, p. 102.

30. *African Worlds, op. cit.*, p. 209.

31. Klah, *op. cit.*, p. 62.

Date Due

24, 77			